MW00635425

Making Sweet Lemonade

Making Sweet Lemonade

By

Pat J. Schulz

www.enheartpublishing.com

Published by ENHEART Publishing
Post Office Box 620086
Charlotte, North Carolina 28262

Copyright © 2007 Pat J. Schulz
Poems throughout this book are written by the author, unless otherwise noted.
Scriptures from The Holy Bible, King James Version.

All rights reserved. No part of this book may be used or reproduced or transmitted in any form or by any means, electronic, mechanical, including photocopying, recording, or by any information storage and retrieval system without written permission from the publisher.

ISBN 0-9654899-6-5
CIP data is available through the Library of Congress
Printed in China

Cover design by Leah Ponds
Layout design by Dan Robinson — TheBooksetter.com

The Lord gave the word; great was the company of those that published it.
Psalm 68:11

More Reviews for

Making Sweet Lemonade

"This was one of the most riveting personal accounts I have read in quite some time. I was moved by the author's willingness to share her pain. I was more impressed, however, by her spiritual development. Clearly, she serves as an inspiration to many and a true testament that life is a journey."

— Carolyn A. Mints
Community Arts Leader

"As a principal, I see many students with the odds against them, but after reading *Making Sweet Lemonade*, I will never give up on working through their struggles. They, too, can beat the odds to become successful just as the author of this phenomenal story."

— Laverne Daniels, EdD
Author, *What Were Those Boys on Bus 40 Thinking?*

"*Making Sweet Lemonade* is a powerful story of a young child's courage to rise above her circumstances and persevere to a life of excellence. The author opens her heart and invites us in to share a very intimate story."

— Joyce B. Sewell
Executive Director, Make a Positive Mpact, Inc.

Dedication

This book is dedicated to all motherless and fatherless children throughout the world. May this story give you hope.

When my mother and father forsake me,
then the Lord will take me up.

— Psalm 27:10

Table Of Contents

Acknowledgements

A life journey simply cannot be traveled alone. The flock you choose will certainly influence the direction of your decisions. For the past twenty years I've been a member of Friendship Missionary Baptist Church (Charlotte, NC), where Dr. Clifford A. Jones, Sr. provides spiritual nourishment through the Word. Over time my soul has cataloged nearly one thousand sermons by Reverend Jones. Those weekly feedings have cumulatively strengthened my spirit for this appointed time.

Amidst the same flock, I stumbled upon a lasting fortress, a friend and counselor in Reverend J.R. Covington, Jr. I went seeking resolve as a grieving mother, yet we unveiled so much more. In the safe confidence of his insight and caring presence, I unraveled the burdens of my heart. Likened to peeling an onion, each layer brought tears of cleansing until we eventually reached the core.

And when the healing is done, there is — more healing. The H.E.A.L.S. Ministry of Friendship Missionary Baptist Church provides a support group of individuals who genuinely care about one another's losses. H.E.A.L.S. has aided my growth into acceptance. Along the same vein, I would also like to acknowledge Sister Therese Galligan and the Bereavement Ministry training team at St. Gabriel Catholic Church (Charlotte, NC) for providing inter-denominational facilitation training — for grief knows no boundaries.

The most important acknowledgement is to the glory of God, the author and creator of every good and perfect gift. This story is His gift to you. I am the vessel.

Introduction

"When life hands you lemons . . . make lemonade."
Chances are you've heard the phrase. Just as there is a process to life and living, there is a process to making lemonade. We start with the core natural product, the lemon. Let's say that's you and me. We are uniquely designed, originating from the earth and genetically coded by a seed. Likewise, each lemon has a distinctive size, shape and density. Beneath its exterior lie essential oils, which are protected from the elements, just as our essence is cloaked in a frame that we call a body. This essence can be our emotions; it can be our innocence; it can be considered our spirit. Our essence is all of these. As we grow and experience life, others attempt to get inside our essence. That becomes the process of building relationships. Are we opening ourselves up to share our beauty and mysteries, or are others taking knives and severing walls to get into our core? This process can be oh, so painful!

In and of itself, the lemon is whole. If nurtured with sunlight, water and good soil it will grow into the fullness for which it was designed. A healthy baby comes into the world equipped with everything needed for its life journey. Experientially, the child is *tabula rasa*, a blank slate. Lessons taught by parents and other care givers teach the child confidence from fear, exploration from apprehension, love from all else. If the child is nurtured in love, then he will grow into the fullness of all he was designed to be. This is a perfect scenario, is it not? It happens, just not for many of us. We grow in spite of others and ourselves. In the process has someone severed your covering, causing your essence to spill out? Did they waste it on a dirty counter? Have the stressors of life weighted against you so long and hard that you could no longer withstand the pressure? Was the essence of your being disturbed and extracted from its once pristine dwelling?

If you can relate to this, all is not lost. Let's think about the person who knows how to carefully prepare a batch of lemonade. They know just the right balance of water, essential oils and sugar to make a succulent batch. When made with love it will be delicious, thirst quenching, each drop savored and appreciated. Keep in mind we cannot omit the lemon or drown out its flavor with too much sugar, else we only have sugar water — something superficial. We must embrace what lemons bring to the table, a unique flavor — a unique experience, if you will.

So, I say again, *"When life hands you lemons, make lemonade."* If this is what is expected of us, I choose to make the *very best* of it. My professional corporate experience groomed one of my best talents — the innate ability to think beyond paradigms and to improve upon that which exists. So it has been as I think upon my life. God has endowed me with intuitive insight, perseverance, exceptional creativity and bountiful faith in order to transform bitter circumstances into joyful living.

This book is comprised of a series of significant events[1] that created a phenomenal spirit of resiliency forming the person whom you will soon read about. However, you may find inklings of yourself or the self you strive to be within the folds of each page. In either case, it is my hope and desire that you will be renewed with a "can-do" spirit.

I've often been regenerated after reading stories of persons who triumphed over life's misfortunes. Over a period of time it became clearer that my life was cataloged among the miracles I read about. I am blessed beyond measure. I've not received all the desires of my heart. *But, when I think upon the goodness of The Lord, and all He's brought me through, I realize my life could have turned out much differently.* This humble acknowledgement settles into my heart when I see a homeless woman on a corner with a sign asking for food, or when I see

---

1   Primarily focused through the formative years

a disabled child, or any myriad of situations as I go about my day. I think, "If not for the grace of God . . ."

This book has been long coming and as of this hour, overdue. I pray God grants mercy upon my soul for my lagging obedience. An individual innocently reminded me that such procrastination is actually disobedience, because our actions, or lack thereof actually say, "I'll do it, Lord, when I get around to it." The adversary has an uncanny way of keeping us busy about nothing. The days pass and we have many reasons and obligations to justify why we couldn't get around to doing the thing that God placed upon our spirit.

One summer day in 2004, I was standing in my kitchen feeling grateful to God for having spared my life — for the *nth* time. A month previously, I had a rapid growing abdominal tumor that required emergency surgery. While being prepped for surgery, I realized something could go awry and I might not awaken from the surgery. Since childhood I've been very familiar with death and therefore, had no fear of it. In fact, there was a time I begged God to take me. I'd completely lost my joy for living. But, He let me continue on this journey and I'm so grateful my joy and fullness for life have since been restored. I knew God had something special for me to do, but that purpose had not been fulfilled.

While on the operating prep table my soul cried out, *"God, I don't want to die. I haven't finished what you called me to do. I need more time, Lord."* By His grace, I awakened from the surgery and healed rapidly. A major surgery that was scheduled for three hours was completed in thirty minutes, without complication. A month later, while standing in my kitchen, the Spirit of the Living God spoke to me, very succinctly, *"It's not for you. It's for others."* I knew exactly what the message was referring to. "It" was my testimony, my life story. "It" is the story that I've protected and kept guarded, but there was a missing. I responded, *"But, who? Who are the others?"*

The others are my kindred brothers and sisters. Those little ones who were physically and emotionally abandoned by their parents, often due to addictions that stripped away their ability to love. Those little ones who are found abandoned in dumpsters and yet survive. Those little ones who ended up in the foster care system and orphanages, or simply passed through to extended family members. Little ones who will never have relationships with their fathers, or *even know* the identity of their natural fathers. Little ones who will become the targets of ridicule and sometimes racism, simply because of whom they were born to.

The heartfelt irony of it all is — those little ones will grow up to become adults. How will they then handle the truth of their being? How do you survive knowing your mother didn't want you? Perhaps she did, but just didn't have the capacity to be a responsible parent. How do you reasonably get along in life without having a constant father figure to benchmark what you ought to look for in a husband? How do you learn to be a man when there was no role model in your household? How do you manage anger (outward-rage) (inward-depression) that you must be responsible for as an adult, but don't understand why, when or how it got there to begin with?

These are the symptoms. Where are the answers? The Lord said, "Suffer little children come unto me."[2] Even though we're all grown up now, God knew us while we were in the womb and the Bible says even before conception.[3] He still sees the little girl and the little boy in us, especially when we seek Him.

In seeking the answer to the truth of my being, God spoke unto my soul, *"It does not matter the medium in which you entered the world. You are my child."* That was not wishful thinking. It was the Spirit of the Living God speaking to me.

And so it is. He spoke it to me and then filled me with the courage to share these words, this story, this life with you. It does not matter the medium in which you entered the

2   Luke 18:16

3   Jeremiah 1:5

world. You are God's child. That knowledge empowers us to overcome the world and all of its maladies. As prevailers, you and I are equipped to take our lumps, pick up our crosses and those baskets of lemons and start "Making Sweet Lemonade."

The Resiliency Theory

The term resiliency has typically been applied to children who overcome acute social conditions such as abuse, neglect, poverty and repeated exposure to violence and go on to lead satisfying, successful lives. These children possess what is considered a *resilient mind-set*. Longevity research indicates resilient children possess characteristics such as excellent problem-solving skills, self-discipline and extraordinary optimism. They recognize their strengths and have a propensity to view mistakes as learning opportunities.

Some consider resiliency an art — the ultimate art of living. At the core of resiliency is an inherent belief in oneself, but also a greater belief in a higher power beyond oneself.

The Man in the Moon

Nighttime can be the scariest time of all for a small child. My mother taught me the light and dark side of night. I saw how life worked on the dark side and never liked what I remembered, so I chose to follow the light.

"Look into the sky. There's the man in the moon." I was no more than three or four when Mama showed me the man in the moon. It was the first wonder of life I remembered and I've marveled ever since. The marvelous thing about the man in the moon is that he is unchanging. No matter where I go, no matter what the day brings, no matter whoever comes into my life and chooses to leave, the man in the moon is always there beaming the face of a gentle comforter. Even when Mama left, he was still there. Of all the lessons she taught me, I am most thankful for being introduced to the man in the moon at an early age, mainly because it made me curious about the wondrous sky? How did it get there? Who made it? What is beyond the moon? All of these questions led me to, of course, God. *God has been my sustainer and the only constant in my life. This is the one truth that can never be taken away.*

Turning Point

A turning point involves a critical decision. When you arrive at a fork in the road you have a decision to make: turn left, turn right, or go straight. Without a map, how do you make a wise decision? You may bet on the chance that if you take the wrong road, you can always turn around and go back to your starting point. Life rarely affords us that opportunity. When you make a decision at the fork in the road, be aware that the turn-around exit may be closed. Choose your turning points wisely. For, not only will these choices direct the course for your life, but also the lives of your children — even those unborn.

A colleague once posed the question, "What was your turning point?" As I pondered the answer to the question, I came to the conclusion there were so many that I could not choose just one. However, for the context of this story I suppose 1968 was a most significant turning point.

After having moved year after year, from Quincy Street to Lexington, Green and Van Buren, my mother and I finally comfortably settled on Bushwick Avenue in Brooklyn, New York. I was in the first grade and life was pretty good. During this phase Mama began a new job at The Little Sisters of Poor convent, and I attended the elementary school across the street. We had a nice little routine. She'd walk me to school every day, and then to work. When school let out, she was waiting outside. When school was closed, I looked forward to going to work with her and spending time with the nuns. I developed a special love and admiration for nuns. They taught me the child's bedtime prayer and gifted me with wonderful keepsakes: a rosary, a pocket bible and framed paintings of the Angel Gabriel, Sister Theresa, now known as Mother or Saint Theresa, and one of Jesus. Each frame was thoughtfully placed on a wall in my bedroom and I spent quiet contemplation with each one daily. Although I had no knowledge or history of Jesus' significance, I would stare at his face and it seemed as though there was a real person looking right back at me. I was especially drawn to the Angel Gabriel, the protector. I wholeheartedly believed this angel was *real* and was placed in my daily presence to specifically protect *me*.

Mama and I did everything together. Some of my fondest memories are of us going to the movies, where Mama would

fill her purse with pizza, hotdogs, canned sodas and sometimes bring fried chicken from home. Every other Saturday
we had our special treat day, which involved an excursion
to an *authentic* Chinese restaurant on Broadway. I was completely engrossed in the nuance of the environment, taking
note of the décor, culture, language and savored the flavor of
authentic sweet and sour pork ribs. On long winter nights, we
cuddled on the couch to watch television. *I Love Lucy* was
my absolute favorite. As far as I was concerned, Lucy could
do no wrong and all her antics were perfectly justified.

I would place Mama's legs across mine while I rubbed them
down with Jergens lotion. The smell of the original Jergens
still reminds me of her. I'd write into the lotion like etching
in sand to see if she could guess the words. I'd squeeze the
pimples from her nose, comb her hair, and meticulously ped-
icure her toes. I'd watch her nap on weekends. If it seemed
she was faking it, I would lift her eyelids and say, "Mama,
are you sleep?" I loved *my* Mama. We were joined at the hip,
especially when both of us needed to use the bathroom at the
same time. She had a habit of taking the newspaper into the
bathroom for long periods. Seeing as we had only one bathroom, I would nudge her over on the seat to tinkle while she
continued reading her paper. We were inseparable.

Daddy would come visit on the weekends. Every Friday he'd
bring us fresh fish. On Saturdays, he'd take me to the movies,

Coney Island, Shea Stadium, shopping and one of my fondest memories — the aquarium. Sometimes we'd just hang out at his garage repair shop on Lexington Avenue. He was a supervisor at the docks in New Jersey and took care of his immigrant Italian mother who spoke no English. Daddy's name was Salbino Agresto, Sal for short. Despite the fact that we lived separately, it seemed to have no bearing on the fact that I loved him and he loved me dearly.

My first great disappointment was the discovery that Sal was not my real father. What was most disheartening was that he began treating me differently. He would still take me out, but his enthusiasm was gone. His heart wasn't in it any longer. It was as if he was just going through the motions. All this came about as a result of showing Daddy my schoolwork. It never occurred to me that my last name, Schulz, was different from his. As a result, he and Mama had an argument. I can still hear his rage as he spoke the words, "She's not my daughter!"

Occasionally, Mama and I would go visit her longtime friend, Ms. Liz. 'Jip' was her nickname. Ms. Liz still lived in the hood, but we had progressed out. Nonetheless, Mama seemed in her element on those once-a-month visits. Part of the trip was to stop by the liquor store to pick up her friend's favorite brand. I was so afraid the bottle would entice my mother to start drinking again.

> Mama stopped drinking after a terrible bout with hallucinations. She'd imagined there were dangerous things in the apartment. I could've been no more than two, but would have visions of the scene as we later discussed the events. She trembled with fear of even the possibility of harming me. She said, "Baby, you looked like a little rabbit to me." She was relieved that she saw me as a harmless rabbit and I was too!
>
> While Mama was in recovery, I stayed with Uncle Eddie and Aunt Margaret Taylor. There were plenty of Uncle and Aunt so-and-so's, who never had any blood ties. Eddie and Margaret doted and adorned me. Margaret didn't work and gave me her undivided attention. We bonded quickly. My favorite pastime was to take the miniature carpet broom she'd bought me and sweep the stairs up and down, over and over. I wanted to be helpful and so enjoy the clean, plush carpet.
>
> I'd also spend quality time with Uncle Eddie's mother, Grandma Taylor. In fact, my relation-

ship with the Taylors began with Grandma Taylor. One of my earliest memories was with Grandma Taylor bathing me in a basin that was uniquely stationed in her bedroom. I can still smell the old-fashioned Oxydol soap. Afterwards, she tucked me into a tightly made bed of fresh, air dried sheets. The room was always dim, not dark, but dim and the ambiance lulled me to sleep.

When Mama got out of rehab, she came for her Baby. Causing a scene on all days, my third birthday — and first party recalled to memory.

The whole day was spent organizing for the party: the cake, the streamers, my dress, my hair, bathing and preparing. Nighttime had just fallen and I was just about to blow out the candles when we heard a commotion outside. "Give me my Baby! I want my Baby. Open this damn door!" That was that. Party was over.

It took a while for Mama to get her act together, but she did. By the end of that summer, we seemed to be on track.

During the early summer of 1968, Ms. Liz visited her people down South. While she was there, she saw Mama's family and reported back, "You should go see your family. Your mother doesn't know if you're alive or dead."

A couple of months later we took our first vacation. The railroad experience was remarkable. From the view, I saw my first countryside, my first unobstructed sunset, my first sight of open green spaces. Every new thing marveled my senses and imagination. We even had our own sleeping quarters and bathroom. The porter brought us breakfast each morning. Oh, that was the life!

Upon our arrival, Mama's family met us at the train station in Hickory, North Carolina and we took a short drive to Lenoir. It was intended to be a short two week vacation, but ended up a nightmare.

Mama was out every night and left me with her mother and sister. I cried endlessly. They thought I was a spoiled brat, but I knew something more. Something or someone was stealing Mama away from me. There was something or someone she'd rather be with than me. I couldn't keep an eye on Mama and I worried what she was doing and with whom.

She'd met up with an old sweetheart. He must have rocked her world, because after that two week vacation, we went back to

New York and packed up our stuff. We were moving to Lenoir and she was getting married. I begged her not to marry him. *"You hardly know this man."* Ah, the wisdom of an eight year old. She knew him when they were young, but many years had passed in between. She didn't know him, but it didn't matter. He must have been pretty convincing. This made me curious about what goes on between a man and a woman that would influence her to do something so radical?

Her plan was to get packed up and gone before Daddy had a clue. But the plan didn't work. Just like clockwork, the Friday after we returned Daddy brought fresh fish, wrapped in newspaper. He was met with a big surprise. Mama was drunk and confronted him on the door step. The bottle didn't entice Mama at Ms. Liz's, but it sure did down in Lenoir. Once she'd gotten it back in her system, there was no turning back.

We left Brooklyn and spent the next year in Lenoir, North Carolina. I enrolled at Harper Elementary for the third grade. Just like in New York, Harper Elementary was integrated. I was totally unaware of the South's racial history and was shielded from the fact that integrated schools were a fairly new phenomenon. I made new friends easily, but especially enjoyed the idea of being part of a family — The Fergusons.

The Fergusons welcomed me. Their disposition toward me was "What took you so long? Where have you been? We've been waiting for you!" Nothing but love!

Mama on the other hand, thought she had found love, but was gravely disappointed. She'd given up so much to be with a man that ended up being her downfall. Before we left New York, I went with Mama to Chase Manhattan Bank to withdraw our accounts. Daddy started a savings account for me. I didn't know how much money was in there, but it was gone now. My mother used all our savings to pay down on an old house out in the country. In that secluded, old country house her new husband beat her down and robbed her of her dignity.

One night, Mama called her brother Raymond out to the country. Her face was bruised, hair frazzled, clothes torn. Uncle Raymond had his pistol and was prepared to use it, if necessary. This was all very unsettling for me. After nine months of this, Mama strategized a method to escape her husband. She secretly told me her plan. She would wait until he was asleep, slip his wallet out of his pocket — after he'd gotten paid, of course — remove the money, get on the bus, go back to New York, find a place for us and then send for me.

Now Mama was smart, but sometimes she did some dumb things. It had to be that thing that happens between a man and a woman, 'cause I never knew my mother to do such a senseless thing as to contact the very man she ran from to ask *him* to place me on the bus. Of course, instead of just taking me to the bus station, he came along also. When we arrived to the destination in Brooklyn, Mama politely said, "Thank you for bringing my Baby." Did she think she would get rid of him that easily?

That summer was hot and dry. I spent the first few weeks sitting in the windowsill observing the neighborhood. I needed to survey the lay of the land before I endeavored to make new friends. From that vantage point, I learned who was who and what was what! Eventually, Mama ordered me out to play. By then I knew who would be my allies and who would not.

> *As I reminisce upon this time, I recognize that I've continued this same assimilation method throughout my life – always quietly assessing the environment before proceeding to assert myself.*

Soon the new school year rolled around and I enrolled in the 4th grade at P.S. 129. This adjustment was harder than the others. We now lived in the heart of the ghetto, eating neck bones instead of fresh fish.

On top of that, the violence escalated now that Mama was completely away from her family. Their volatile relationship often put me in a nervous state. Police would come, but no action was taken. They deemed it a "family dispute." On one particular occasion the two were arguing publicly. I could sense the rage rising. All of a sudden, Mama grabbed my hand and started running. I thought she was running to escape John. As we ran across the street, she threw us both face down onto the ground, into the middle of the street, in the path of oncoming traffic. Now, mind you the traffic light was red and cars were stopped at the light, but this was insane!

I later suspected it was a ploy to gain his sympathy, but remember thinking, *'If you want to die that's your choice, but don't take me with you.'* Thank God, we were spared of being rolled over. When I was let up a million thoughts ran through my head. I especially thought back to just a year previously and how different our lives were. Little did I know, the worst of times were ahead.

In the Summer Time

A year passed and another summer's onset seemed to bring new hope. Sometime in mid-June of 1970, I set out on a joyful early morning walk to school. The trek to Gates and Stuyvesant was one I footed daily. After weathering the winter, the walk on a sunny morning was quite delightful. It was the last day of school and I wore my favorite dress, a red, white and blue navy flap dress. Despite the fact that our living conditions were not as bountiful as they once were, Mama still had a knack for finding me nice things.

We had a party at school that day and my spirits were light. As I walked back home, I noticed something un-usual. Somebody's furniture was out on the street. Mama was waiting outside for me. We'd been evicted. Every day was an unexpected event it seemed, even on the best of days. With the optimistic spirit of those who know how to take a bitter situation and extract something positive, I thought, *'I'm so glad I wore my favorite dress. At least I get to keep this one.'* That was all I got to keep. Everything else remained on the street. Having all our belongings on the curb for public display was painfully embarrassing. I was tired of Mama putting me in embarrassing situations.

John went his way and we went ours. I thought, *'This is a good thing. We can be rid of him now.'* Mama had a plan. I didn't know what it was, but you can be sure I was asking questions. She was quick to tell me not to talk so much, and even popped me in the mouth once or twice to teach me the lesson. I never thought that was an effective way to teach the lesson. It didn't squelch my curiosity about life or human behavior. I constantly begged the question, "Why?" This time the question was "Where?" Where will we go?

Mama had some old faithful friends on Quincy Street — Mr. Percy Sutton and his wife. I didn't remember them, but they seemed to know me well. The Suttons provided temporary residence until Mama could work out further arrangements. Even though we lived upstairs, I spent most of my time exploring with the Suttons.

The Suttons had an organ in their living room that I was naturally drawn to. It beckoned me. Apparently, I had a natural talent for the keys. I remember as a younger child having requested a keyboard for Christmas, and taught myself songs like, "Twinkle, Twinkle, Little Star." In addition, during my stay in Lenoir an elderly neighbor, Ms. Gussie, gave me piano lessons. She said I had the right fingers for the craft and lauded the fact that I could naturally lock up my joints. I took that to mean I had something special and desirous in order to become an avid pianist.

Now I had a chance to relearn the keys. Didn't take long. I had plenty of focused time without interruption. It was summer, no school and nowhere to go. I liked that! When Mama wanted to take me with her in the streets, the Suttons said, "No, let her stay with us." I loved the sense of comfort and ease in the Sutton home.

Mrs. Sutton gave me a couple of good lessons on *My Wild Irish Rose*, and I played it over and over until the pace was perfected. I don't remember how I knew the song at all. It was not a common song and very outdated for the era.

Nonetheless, *My Wild Irish Rose* was my choice selection and before long I mastered the organ — mostly on my own.

It would not be until my later adult years that I would learn of a grandmother named Rose (albeit she was not Irish) and that she was masterful at the piano. Could it have been I subconsciously remembered the tune, having listened to her play as an infant?

As life has rapidly moved along, one of the things I've learned about myself is that I have an uncanny sensory memory. Modern day theory deems this a component of emotional intelligence.

Another connection came later in life. I was watching 'Live at the Apollo' late one night and saw the trailer Percy Sutton, Sr., Producer, scroll by big as day. Although I'd watched the show many times before, this time the name registered like the rising of the sun. I wondered, *'could it be?'* I recalled Ms. Liz, telling me the two used to party in Harlem in the post WWII hay-days. It was the place to be. So, I just wondered . . . could it be? I suppose it could very well be.

Even though I enjoyed my time with the Suttons, I was concerned about all the clothes I'd lost. Since I can remember,

I've always been particular about clothing. I don't know if this was a conditioned behavior or an innate preference.

> When I found out about Grandmother Rose, I also learned about her father. My great-grandfather was an excellent custom tailor – one of the finest. So, perhaps my preference in fine couture could have been genetically coded.

All I know is one of my early memories is of going to Lerner's specialty shop. I was so small, I could only see upon the bottom rack, which was really low for little ones. Mama said, "Pick out the one you like." I carefully gazed upon the row of frilly dresses. They all looked like doll dresses to me. I picked the one I liked. According to Mama, it was the most expensive on the rack. That day I got my choice, but it wasn't always that way.

Mama gave the impression we were going to start a new life without John, but one day she got lonely. She asked me to go see John and give him a message. Seems like it was a coded message. In order to relay the message, I had to walk from Quincy Street to Lexington and Throop, which was about eight city blocks. There wasn't anything I wouldn't do for Mama. So I went on my late afternoon walk, while enjoying the autonomy. By the time I got there it was dusk and John was shocked to see me. He sent me back by bus. I gave Mama his message and she sent me back walking, this time in the dark. There was a particular block that didn't seem too friendly when I went by the first time. I'd gotten a lot of intense stares, but I kept my head up and looked ahead. But, when I came by the second time, I knew my odds were beginning to run thin. So, I picked up the pace and got out of Dodge as fast as I could.

Surprisingly, no one bothered me. I suppose my protective angel was with me.

> I've read accounts of situations where, for example, a robber was about to take someone down, but hesitated because "that big guy was there." However, in a physical sense the individual was alone.

"Make yourself familiar with the angels, and behold them frequently in spirit; for without being seen, they are present with you."

— *St. Francis de Sales*

When I showed up the second time, John was infuriated with Mama for sending me out by myself in the dark. It certainly did put me in the risk of danger. He sent me back again by bus. When I saw his concern for my safety, I thought, '*He's not such a bad guy.*' I began to trust him more, despite the harm he'd already brought to Mama.

Prior to this he didn't know where we were staying, but apparently it was her intention that he know, so I told him. A few hours later he showed up and called her from the street to come out. I could see his fury and begged her not to go. Nonetheless, she went outside. He called her every 'stupid bitch' name a person could think of and then some. The name-calling was embarrassing, but what followed was devastating. I watched from a third story window as he grabbed her hair and jerked her so hard you could see her neck snap. Looked like an NFL face mask penalty. Unfortunately, there were no referees. That wasn't the end of it. My heart sank into my stomach as he rammed her head into what appeared to be one of the largest oak trees I've ever seen. I yelled, "Stop! Stop it! Leave my Mama alone!" My pleas fell on deaf ears. My small voice was lost in the rage. Mama was slapped, battered and bammed to a pulp that night.

As a result of her poor judgment and inviting a violent situation onto the Sutton's property, she was ousted. That meant I had to go too. Guess where we ended up next? Yep, that's right, back with her husband.

Disciples Sent Two By Two

John worked with two brothers who owned a mom and pop moving company. They also had a used furniture store. Unclaimed furniture was stacked up in the front of the building. In the back there were two rooms and a bathroom with no shower or tub — just a basin and toilet. This is where John found refuge upon the eviction. This pseudo furniture store became our homestead for the next year. Did I say I was tired of Mama putting me in embarrassing situations? This topped the list.

Ever see Spike Lee's movie *Crooklyn*? If so, do you recall the characters constantly sitting out on their stoops? That's because there was no air conditioning on the inside. It was sweaty hot! We didn't have a stoop, but the brothers would place chairs outside the storefront and we would sit outside eating watermelon to cool off, while I wished for someone to pop the fire hydrants. The brothers were kind, respectable men. Based upon their respectability, I began to think most men were like them — wouldn't do a thing to harm a child. That was a fallacy.

The summer passed and the new school year began. I was in the fifth grade and had a new teacher, Mr. Wachs. He wasn't anything like my fourth grade teacher, Ms. Brenda Cooper. Wachs seemed to have it out for me. I had to write sentences upon sentences, until it became sheer punishment. Why was I called out so much? Generally, someone would say something to me. I'd respond and get caught. I was always the one getting caught talking in class. I'd just begun to make friends and he was cutting off my social growth. Not to mention, I was still recovering from a hellacious fourth grade transition and had to start over with the same group of kids, some who tortured me the year before. I couldn't afford to give them anything new to pick at me about.

Mama warned if the teacher called her to school, she would pull my pants down and spank me in front of the whole class. The worse thing would be to let everyone see my behind. I would never recover if that happened.

The first week Mama walked me to school. On the way, we happened upon Denise, a girl that used to live in our building when we were on Gates Avenue. Denise was the biggest girl I'd ever met. For today's standards she would have been the Shaquille O'Neal of the fifth grade girls, and thank God for it! Mama asked her to keep an eye on me and help out if anyone tried to pick a fight with me. Denise was good about that, but she wasn't around all the time.

The bully in our class was Barry and for some reason he decided he would 'jump' me after school. I was the smallest one in the class and the fairest thing in school. Next to William, a goggled eyeglass wearing kid, I was a most unusual misfit. I suppose that gave them license to pick on me. Their disdain for my skin color was heightened after we began weekly Afro-American History classes, where together we all learned about slavery. It was the first time I heard about the plight of Africans to America via the slave trade. Even though I was learning this history lesson along with my other classmates, they began to take the issues out on me, as if I should bear responsibility for hundreds of years of enslavement . . . this was the instigation behind the battle.

Initially, I was not a skilled fighter and inept at protecting myself. I quickly learned I could kick in a swift sprint. Mama said running was the worst thing to do. Even if it meant getting beat, I had to stand my ground. It was an early lesson about survival of the fittest in ghetto life. There was another early survival lesson. Sometimes people don't have a valid

47

reason against *you*. If they feel like blowing off some steam and if you're an easy target — look out!

> To solve the issue of being an easy target, I decided to request a conference with the Afro-American History teacher. I explained that her lessons were *causing me problems*. The kids were taking their frustrations out on me. I was not there. I didn't have anything to do with slavery. So, why should I take the brunt of an entire history before me? Her lessons initiated the conflict and I needed her to straighten it out. She did, but in the meantime . . .

People gathered around as if there were going to be an Ali vs. Joe Frasier round. I was wondering how I would escape the madness without injury. It was not looking favorable for me.

Right then, before a finger was laid on my precious little body, two women appeared out of nowhere. "Why are you bothering that little girl? No, you're not going to do anything." They spoke with authority that diffused the situation and rebuked the devils that were seeking to devour me.

That day I met my earthen angels, Evangelist F. C. Fisher and Evangelist Pearl Kemp. They'd just completed some mission work and were led to take a different route back home to Dean and Kingston. Being concerned for my safety, Sister Fisher and Sister Kemp went further out of their way to walk me home. A couple of blocks away from where we stayed, I said *"I'll be OK from here."* But, they wouldn't hear of it. They wanted to make sure I got home safely. Reluctantly, I led them to the used furniture store. We walked into the back where Mama was and they introduced themselves — God's Agents.

A week later, the Sisters came back and invited us to church. When Mama declined the invitation, they asked if she would mind if they took me along to church. I was already drawn to their loving spirits and wanted to spend more time with them.

I think my mother was more inclined than usual to let me go because I was suffering with bursitis, which was lodged in my neck. The cold was imbedded so deeply, I could not turn my neck. We had previous experience with the miraculous power of prayer.

> Around age five, I began having uncontrollable nosebleeds. Mama tried all sorts of home remedies, including ice packs on my forehead, stuffing my nostrils and placing strips of brown paper bag along my gum line. When her rem-

edies failed, she called upon a neighbor on Van Buren Street. The neighbor read a verse from the Bible, prayed on me and anointed my head with oil. Within minutes the bleeding stopped.

So . . . Mama let me go with Sister Fisher and Sister Kemp in hopes their prayers would heal my neck.

That weekend at Zion Church of Christ I witnessed Godly faith in action and was introduced to The Lord Jesus Christ. Over the subsequent months, I spent more and more time at 1405 Dean Street, where the church was housed on the ground level. Sister Fisher and Sister Fields had apartments on the second floor and Sister Kemp lived on the top floor with her two boys, Ronnie and Roger. I looked forward to my time with the Sisters, Ronnie, Roger and members of the church. Collaboratively, they all provided a healthy, balanced environment, where not only was my spirit nurtured, but so were my mind and body. Sister Fisher had libraries of books for countless hours of learning. Ronnie and Roger were competitive in Word Power and other board games. They let me play with them. It was rare that I came close to beating them, but I loved the competition and it fed my desire to master the meaning of words. During my absence, I would study the words I'd missed so I would be more knowledgeable for the next game. I think I surprised those guys a time or two. They were gracious to allow me to share their mother during my visits. Sister Kemp fed us well. She was a good listener, a good hugger, overall just a really great mother. One of the things I especially enjoyed was taking long, soaking hot baths while in Sister Kemp's care. Even though the bathroom supported three other people, Sister Kemp never rushed me out. She offered a private solace that I looked forward to. For that time, I was the little princess of the abode.

Sister Fisher was the pastor of the church and what an orator! Not only was she a dynamic minister, but also an independent real estate owner. At times I would go with Sister Fisher to collect rent and boy she did not play. With the same authority that commanded the bully to let me be, she collected her monthly payments. Tenants respected Frances Fisher, woman of God. They all provided tidbits that strengthened my resolve to cope with whatever awaited me upon my return back to Mama. But, accepting Jesus Christ as my Lord and Savior was the most powerful, long lasting and meaningful experience.

One night back at the furniture store I was caught up in prayer, asking God for the gift of the Holy Ghost. I knew if I were to survive life, I would need the power of the Holy

Spirit to keep me pure and out of danger.

> *Even though Sister Fisher and Sister Kemp couldn't be with me every hour of the day, the Holy Spirit could. I'd witnessed it in their lives and even in the lives of some of the young people in the church and wanted to be drawn closer to God.*

I was on my knees in my private space, that we called a room. I'd gotten so caught up in prayer that tears were streaming down my face as I petitioned God for the anointing of the Holy Spirit.

I was alarmed by a voice in the doorway. Seems as if I was in a trance, because the figure and the words being spoken weren't clear at first. Then I realized it was Mama demanding that I stop praying. An automatic response came from me retorting, *"I will not stop praying. It's only the devil in you trying to make me stop praying. I rebuke you Satan in the name of Jesus."* She turned away and walked out.

I remained on my knees praying, but saddened that I had been interrupted from the closest spiritual experience I'd shared with God. I was also saddened to know there was so much to be wary of out in the world; yet awakened to the fact that I was living with the enemy.[4]

The enemy had consumed Mama. I began to see people and relationships with people as pawns in spiritual warfare.

You would think because I had to learn the lesson so early that I would have been so much further along in deliverance. Well, to my dismay, I've been deceived and side tracked more than I would like to admit.

> *Nonetheless, from time to time throughout my youth Sister Fisher reminded me how I'd written a little boy in Haiti on how he could be saved. She simply planted the seeds to say, if you fall by the wayside, you know your way back.*

I thank God every day for sending Sister Fisher and Sister Kemp into my life. Their lives have remained with me as benchmarks of true Christian faithfulness and integrity. When I met them I was just ten years old and we remain close even today. I often hear Sister Fisher's loving reminders, *"Tomorrow is not promised, dear Pat. Seek The Lord today. Don't be conformed to the ways of the world, for it will surely pass. Only what you do for God will last."*

---

4   Matthew 10:36

Put on the whole armour of God,
that ye may be able to stand against
the wiles of the devil.
For we wrestle not against flesh and blood,
but against principalities, against powers, against rulers
of darkness of this world,
against spiritual wickedness in high places.

— Ephesians 6:11-12

My Shawshank

I walked into the back of the pseudo furniture store, looking for Mama to tell her about school that day.

"Where's Mama?" I asked John.

"She went across the street," he replied.

John had been drinking. It had gotten to the point where I couldn't judge if his drinking was celebratory for a good work week, or a pity party for a bad work week. Nonetheless, he seemed to be in a good mood, but reflective.

He said, "Come over here. I want to tell you something. You can sit on my lap."

John proceeded to tell me the he loved me like his own daughter. As he told me this, his hand went under my dress and I thought he was going to pat me on the behind. That was something Mama would do a lot. But, something different happened. His hand went to a place that Mama never touched. When I began pulling back, he pressed me against him and put his mouth to mine and then tried to thrust his tongue into my mouth. Mama kissed me on the lips, but she never put her tongue into my mouth. I pressed my lips tighter and pulled away until I broke free.

I didn't know what to think. Mama told me about the dangers of talking to strangers or accepting candy or money from them, but this caught me off guard. I retreated to my private space and into myself. He followed into the room, begging me not tell Mama. I was considering not telling her, but all of a sudden she showed up out of nowhere. As she walked up, he was walking out. Mother's instincts always know. She grabbed my arm, "Come on. Let's go." Her stride was motivated by sheer adrenalin, as we whisked by John and out the door.

We walked up and down the block as she interrogated me. "What was he doing in your room? What did he say? Did he do anything to you?" I could not lie to Mama. She'd torn my butt up a time or two when she even suspected I'd lied. I knew her consequences would be much worse than anything he'd done.

After she asked the same questions over and over and I gave her the same answers over and over. She grabbed my hand

and we were off to the police station. The precinct looked just like a scene from *NYPD Blue*. The detectives wrote down everything I said and unlike with Mama, I didn't have to repeat it a million times. They believed me the first time.

We escorted the police back to the scene to identify John. I watched him being arrested and that very night we went to court. How we arrived to the courthouse is a blur, I do not remember. I suppose it had to have been by police car, *which helps me to better understand my anxiety of police cars.*

In the corridor of the majestic downtown Brooklyn courthouse, Mama proceeded to interrogate me again. I kept telling her the same story over and over. She was getting out of control and it was making me nervous. Mama took me aside, where no one could see us and told me I had to say I'd made it all up. I was so confused. Why would she take me to the precinct to have charges filed and then rescind? I questioned her. She slapped me so hard that I thought my face would fall off. I knew my face was red, 'cause it stung like fire. In that instant, my love for her dissolved. She wasn't trying to protect me. She was more concerned about what would happen to him. The police told her the seriousness of the crime. He was facing twenty years in jail.

At the point of impact, innate survival instincts kicked in. *I was in danger.* I began evaluating my surroundings. I surveyed the long halls for exit doors. How could I escape? Could I run fast enough? Yes, but then what? Where would I go? I was in unfamiliar territory. If I didn't go along, I'd have to go back home with her and what would be my consequence for noncompliance? If I went along with the lie, he would be set free and I'd have to go back home with him. Either way, the odds weren't satisfactory.

We were called into court. I was hoping the judge could see her finger print on my face and order me into safe custody. My eyes pleaded to him to read the cries of my heart, but my mouth was in contradiction. Mama said, "She made it all up." When asked to confirm, the consequences raced through my head. Even though I wanted to be removed, my greatest fear was foster care. To avoid what seemed to be the greater of two evils, I nodded *yes*. I could see the judge's reluctance. Nonetheless, the case was dismissed.

That night the three of us left on the bus back "home." I looked out the window and would not acknowledge either of the two cowards. I was betrayed by two people who both claimed they loved me.

> *Perhaps this was my first hard-core lesson that real love is evidenced not by what people say, but what they do.*

She tried to make it right with me by settling with John that he had to go away in exchange for having spared his life in jail. He complied, but none to soon — two weeks later he left. Instead of John being sentenced, I was. Being forced to live with my personal assailant — a child molester — was imprisonment. Even though I had to be present sharing the same living space, I was not there. I'd developed the ability to selectively block out deterrents and repress my emotion.

As I think on this situation, it reminds me of how much I've appreciated the film, *Shawshank Redemption.*

> *Even though we have been limited in space, place and freedom for a time, we will not allow our minds and spirits to be chained.*

Hunter College

Another summer was upon us. It's interesting how the seasons become so important. Natural elements are balanced by seasonal changes. I remember events by seasons. My mood and energy levels change with the seasons. In the summer of 1971, I entered into a whole new season in my life. My innocence was gone and neither was Mama the same. Her intentions were to protect me from harm, but it happened in an instant.

If you've been following along closely, you must surmise we were homeless, yet again. Where would we go this time? Familiar territory usually reigns supreme. We initially shared space with some of my mother's errant cohorts. Just as a bird searches for twigs to build a safe nesting place, I watched as Mama went about her mission, politicking to locate a comfortable homestead. By means of default, we obtained our own one bedroom apartment on Gates and Reid Avenue, now renamed Malcolm X Blvd.

I suppose Mama saw the change in me, as well. I could no longer trust her to take care of me. Our bond had been broken and as far as I was concerned, I was on my own. There began a role reversal process. I took on household and caretaking responsibilities, for not only myself, but for Mama also. She began leaving me alone in the apartment and that was just fine with me. As long as I didn't let anyone into the apartment, it was a safe place and I was content.

Beginning a new school year is generally an exciting time for children, because that means back-to-school shopping. To make up for a barren Christmas, Mama awarded me with a bountiful back-to-school excursion. However, the real fun was the opportunity and test to go *solo*. I wanted a pair of Levi jeans and a pair of newly in style platform shoes, as well as school staples. Mama needed some things too. She asked me to find her a 36C bra and some household goods. With a wad of cash, I set out to Broadway on a shopping excursion. My self-imposed objectives were first and foremost to be discrete. So, I split the money up into different pockets. Therefore, when I paid for an item, I did not expose the full amount of money. I also wanted to maximize my purchasing power with the resources in hand, and surprise Mama with a little something extra. I attained all my goals. I found everything I wanted to begin back-to-school; the 36C bra; everything else on the list and a bonus surprise for Mama. I combined bags to conceal most of the goods and was on the bus well before dusk.

From the outside looking in one might say my mother had become quite neglectful. However, being thrust into taking on such responsibility advanced my self confidence and instilled a realization that the same confidence could be applied toward social skills.

Anticipating the new school year, I came to the realization that *you can't go about things the same way and expect different results.*

Therefore, I needed to do some things differently to ensure I didn't fall into the same vulnerable traps. So, I made a conscientious decision to cut my hair *off.* Long hair became a handicap in battle. It blocked the peripheral vision and thereby was easier to be blind-sided. From a child's perspective, there is nothing more frustrating than having your hair pulled by someone you cannot see. I also came to the realization that a plan of action was *mandatory.* Just as one sets New Year's resolutions, I set new school year resolutions. The hair was the first on the list. I consulted with Mama on this decision. After stating my case, she had no arguments against cutting the hair. *Chop! Chop!* Eleven years of growth was gone!

Secondly, I realized I needed to project myself as the aggressor, and envisioned the likelihood of coming forth as the victor. Even though I still hadn't grown much and remained one of the smallest kids in my grade, survival instincts overshadowed the height deficiency. In fact, my newfound confidence made me forget I had a height deficiency.

I selected my opponent, a tall slender classmate named Vivian. She was someone whom I felt needed to be avenged for past offenses. Just as I envisioned: the bell rang, the crowd gathered and cheered, but this time some were rooting for me. I executed victoriously and was crowned with a robe of newfound respect. I wondered why it took me so long to figure out the formula, and some of my classmate's non-verbals suggested the same. No one bothered me again, but just in case, I packed a razor in my pencil case. Now that I'd demonstrated the physical ability to handle a scuffle I was determined to come full throttle, if ever intimidated again.

> This scenario helps us relate to juvenile offenders and even gang mentality. Given my circumstances, I would have been the ideal individual drawn to the protection of a gang.

Thanks be to God, I was blessed with the ultimate protector
— The Holy Spirit.

The winter was cold and brutal. I knew times were at their worst when I awakened on Christmas morning to no tree, decorations or gifts — not one. We pretended it was just another Sunday morning. As a matter of routine, I gathered some change to pick up Mama's *Daily News* and breakfast, two egg sandwiches at the local corner store. Also, as a matter of routine I stopped downstairs to see if our elderly neighbor needed anything from the store. When I returned, she gave me a red purse. I cherished that red purse. It was my only Christmas gift. It was obvious we'd hit hard times. On more than one occasion our lights were disconnected. We cooked with Sterno cans and read by candlelight. I remember smelling my hair sizzling into a candle flame while leaning over brushing my teeth one morning. From an economic standpoint, it was evident Mama was struggling without a helpmate.

> I think this is when I declared I would not be dependent on anyone for my livelihood. I would make my own way, *earnestly*. I could not allow myself to be left penniless or tolerate abuse, because I needed someone to keep a roof over my head and the lights on. *Even though I loved school, I had not quite made the connection that education would be the key to my independence.*

After such a dreadful holiday, I couldn't wait for school to commence. School provided a purpose and an escape. If I could've stowed away a cot in my classroom, I would have. In fact, I daydreamed many a day on such a thing.

But in my wildest daydreams, I could not have imagined the opportunity of a lifetime that awaited in the new semester. Because of previous aptitude test scores, I was one of five students selected to test for a college placement program at Hunter College in Manhattan. The five girls formed a bond as we coached one another while preparing for the test. I put additional attention to my homework and further developed my skill to block out distracting forces, Mama in particular. I needed to remain focused.

The night before the test, I asked Mama to wake me up early to ensure I did not miss my ride to Manhattan. Darlene's parents agreed to let me ride with them to Hunter College. Testing began at 8:30 a.m. and we had to leave at 7:00 o'clock. That meant I had to get up at 6:00 o'clock. This was the *one* time I needed Mama to resume her duties and *help me* be prepared. I still feel the disappointment, recalling how I felt when I awakened at 7:00 o'clock and fought my way across the ice and snow to get to Darlene's house, hoping by some ray of benevolence they were waiting for me. But, they were not. To say I was frustrated would be an understatement. Frustration turned to anger, primarily toward my mother and that energy propelled me over the ice and snow to get to school as quickly as possible. My motive was to ask, no beg, the principal to take me to Hunter College. Do you know Mr. Pratt had the nerve to tell me he could not!? And do you know I had the nerve to tell him, he *had* to!? I would not settle for anything less than, "Well, OK."

Persistence, my friend, is well . . . my friend.

After pleading and crying, and crying and pleading, Mr Pratt agreed to drive me to Hunter College for testing. After having worked so diligently, I just could not let this opportunity pass me by.

It was 9:00 o'clock when we arrived and the students were already testing. I cannot tell you I wasn't nervous, I was. I realized I was already behind, but I had plenty of trial practice toward mastering the ability to block out externals in order to focus. So, I settled down, took a deep breath, forgot about Murphy's Law and took that test!

Perseverance —

to continue steadfastly[5]

5   Oxford American Dictionary

February 26

February 26, 1972 was a Sunday. The Saturday before, Mama and I went to Ms. Kat's apartment on the corner of Stuyvesant and Gates Avenue. I was very familiar with Ms. Kat and the company she kept. I really didn't want to go, but had no say in the decision. We left early in the day. Once we arrived at Ms. Kat's place I knew what to expect. They drank liquor and played cards all day and all night. Usually the same characters would show up at Ms. Kat's house. This day, there was someone new. There was a young woman who sat by herself, sucking her thumb while she rocked back and forth. I asked, "Why is she doing that?" Mama said, "because of something she missed," *as in didn't get when she was younger*. I prayed whatever she didn't get that caused her to rock uncontrollably, with thumb in mouth, was not the same thing I'd missed. Instinctively, I knew I had also missed out on something, but didn't know what it was.

As the day got late, I began to get sleepy and nudged Mama. I was ready to go. For some reason she was relentless about staying, continuing to drink and play cards. She demanded I just go to sleep on the couch, lying behind her. I tried to go to sleep. Lord knows, I tried. Normally, nothing would keep me from falling off to sleep, not the lights, nor the loud talking, nothing. But, there was an odor I could not contend with. I'm not talking about stinky arms. I mean a dreadful stench. I wondered, '*Am I the only person here who smells this awful odor?*' I tried to determine from where it was coming. Going through the process of elimination, I concluded it was Mama emitting the nasty odor. How embarrassing! But more so, it made me want to throw up. I couldn't handle it. Yet, she made me lie there behind her. At one point it seemed as though she was pressing me against the back of the couch, to be sure I didn't move.

Another 24 hours would pass before I'd realize what I experienced up close and personal was the onset of death, via blood cell deterioration. Unfortunately, Mama had numbed her body, deluged with alcohol. I can only presume she was unaware of the full impact of her pain.

Finally, yielding to my squirming and persistent pleas to leave, we headed home. We lived only 1½ blocks away, but it was the longest road we traveled together. It took us an hour to get home. This night the street was desolate and covered with glassy ice. On a late frigid Saturday night in Bed-Stuy even the hoodlums were keeping warm and all the children were nestled snug in their beds, except for me.

As we slowly walked that quarter mile, Mama seemed quite tentative in her steps. We walked arm in arm to support one another from slipping on the ice, but it seemed I was holding on closer and tighter to keep her secure. She told me she was sick and that her vision in one eye had been blurry for a while. I surmised as a result of the beatings she'd endured.

> In particular, my mind raced back to the day Mama showed up at school unexpectedly. I was called out of class to the principal's office and knew something was wrong. She was waiting for me there, wearing a pair of Jackie Onassis sunglasses. When she took the shades off, my heart sank into my stomach. Her left eye was completely blood shot and she said she'd been hit in the head. There was a laceration on her scalp. Mama took me out of school that day. She needed the one thing she could draw love and strength from. She needed me.

I begged Mama to go to the hospital, but she quickly replied, "Who would take care of you? I can't leave my Baby." After she'd gotten me back from the Taylors', from there on she

71

was overly protective of leaving me with anyone. I said, "I can stay with Miss Bert," our downstairs neighbor. She never said another word about it.

About that time she slipped on the ice. I was so afraid she'd gotten hurt. I tried to help her up, but she refused my help — admonishing that such an attempt would cause me to fall also. I really thought by leaning on me, she would be able to lift herself up. However, she knew she could not. She was weak. I obviously did not understand the full extent of her condition.

As I said, the road was desolate. No one was walking the streets that night and only a few passers by car. I yelled for help to each one, but they passed us by. Finally, there came a crowd of three or four teenage boys. We were leery of crowds of teenage boys at night in the ghetto, but I had to take a chance. We had no options. I yelled, "Please help us. Help my Mama."

"Oh, that 'ole drunk woman."

I pleaded, "No, she's not drunk. She's sick. Please help us." They hesitated, but eventually came over and lifted her up. Now, we could finish our journey home.

When we got to our apartment building I was relieved, but

we had four flights of stairs to climb. Mama couldn't make it to the top of the first set before she stumbled again. Seems like it was midnight now. I dreaded knocking on doors, waking people up, but in this case . . .

The first apartment entering the building was Mr. Johnson's, the superintendent. I knocked. "Mr.Johnson can you let us stay with you for the night? My Mama is sick and she can't make it up the stairs. Please let us stay. I don't know what else to do." He befriended us and Mama had a place to be comfortable and sleep away her inebriation.

The next morning I was awakened by the sound of children. That was unusual. I heard children playing, trying to be quiet because someone was sleeping in the next room, but of course, they were not. The sound of their laughter enticed me, and I was curious about what they were doing. It sounded like so much fun. These were Mr. Johnson's grandchildren visiting. So, I slipped out of bed with Mama and went into the other room to meet the children and play.

After a while, Mama called me and I went to see about her. She was sweating and asked for water. I got Mama the glass of water and stayed with her a while. She asked me to stay with her and not leave. Soon she dozed back off to sleep. I slipped away to go back into the other room to be with the children. But, my spirit became weary and I sat on the couch, looking out the window wondering what I could do for Mama. I told Mr. Johnson, "My Mama is sick and needs to go to the hospital." He seemed unalarmed, believing she was more drunk than sick, or just sick from being drunk. Mr. Johnson didn't have a telephone. I asked him to give me a dime, so I could go across the street to make a call. He didn't have a dime.

Mama called me again. This time she wanted a cup of coffee. As I poured the water into the pot to heat for coffee, I leaned over the sink in complete helplessness and began to pray with tears in my eyes, "*Dear God, please don't let my Mama die.*" I believed in the power of prayer and left Mama in God's hands.

In obedience, not knowing if the coffee was good for her, or not, I gave Mama her cup of coffee. We talked for a little while and I asked her if I could go back to play. It was so rare for me to play with other children. I wanted to seize the opportunity while it was available. Then we heard a thump. Mama had fallen off the bed onto the floor. I thought, '*Mama is sleeping hard today. She needed the rest. We were out late the night before.*' We picked her up and placed her back on the bed. A while later "thump" again and one of Mr. Johnson's granddaughters came in the playroom shouting, "That lady's dead! That lady's dead!" I yelled back, "You shut up! I will knock you through the wall if you say it again. You don't know what you're talking about. She's asleep."

Then I leaned down to examine Mama. I've seen her asleep a million times. I was the expert on Mama. I knew her inside and out. *Let me see. I will tell you what's going on with Mama.* I rolled her over from her side to her back. The first thing I looked at was her eyes. They were half open. Mama never slept with her eyes half open. Then I noticed Mama's mouth was filled with blood. Then, her lips — they were blue. Then, her skin — it was pale blue. I didn't cry right then. I just said, "Mama never sleeps with her eyes open. She must be dead."

In less than a minute another neighbor came in, who happened to be a *nurse*. In less than five minutes time the police were there pulling me away from Mama and asking questions. I told them the same, "Mama must be dead. She never sleeps with her eyes open." They took me outside. I looked up and there was a crowd of people. In the crowd there was Tony, Cowboy and Mr. Ray, all men that once cared about Mama. '*How did they hear about this so soon?*' They were all crying, side by side. I remembered thinking, '*if they cared about her this much, why didn't they stay with her? Why were they only in her life a short time?*' Her husband had long gone, back to Carolina, or somewhere. Who knew?

It was all happening so fast, but thoughts were running through my head. *I should have done more. I should have left to make the phone call. But, I didn't want to not be there, if she needed me. I knew Mama was sick, but didn't know she was this*

75

close to death. I thought what she needed was sleep. Mr. Johnson could have done more.

It blew my mind that we had a nurse in our building. *Why didn't I know that? And she had a telephone, no less. Why didn't Mr. Johnson go to her when I told him Mama was sick and needed an ambulance?*

Why didn't God answer my prayer? I'd been a good girl. Why wouldn't He honor my prayer?

The fact that God did not answer my prayer and let Mama die numbed me. I continued to love the Lord, but now felt prayer was futile. "What will be, will be," just like Doris Day sang. God has determined it all, and you can pray all you want. If it's not in His will, you are wasting your time.

This tragedy could have been avoided if they . . . if I . . . if . . .

But, something eventually told me Mama was tired. She'd given up. She probably had been sick for a long time. Mama lost hope a long time ago. That made me so sad.

The police asked whom should they call for me. It was the first time I felt protected by the police. I didn't know what was going to happen to me — hadn't given it any consideration. But, the fact they left the choice to me made me feel grown up. I was also grateful they would not be taking me to foster care or an orphanage. It was one of those split minute decisions. Sal, the man I once adored and believed was my father, crossed my mind, but I wasn't sure. Uncle Raymond came to mind and I felt the warmth of his love all in my body just imagining being in his presence. Without hesitancy I said, "Call Raymond Ferguson in Lenoir, North Carolina."

I was then asked to let the police into our apartment, but could not find the keys. Somewhere along the way Mama lost our keys. The police had to use special equipment to get the door unbolted. There seemed to be such a fiasco all over the building. After so much time passed I realized *Mama is gone. I never saw them take her away.*

Once the door was finally unlocked I was able to get some things, but I felt rushed and I kept thinking, *'Mama is gone and I didn't see them take her away.'* It was all beginning to settle in. I wanted to cry then, but couldn't. I wanted to stay in the apartment a while and process it all, but they were rushing me. I wasn't able to get all the things I wanted to. Besides, I had no suitcase to pack them in. Among a few belongings I was able to take was my new poster and typewriter, given to me by Vivas; the red purse — my only Christmas gift that year; a half slip Sister Kemp gave me; a colorful winter jacket Sister Fisher gave me; and my King James Bible, also given to me by Sister Fisher. These were all my favorite keepsakes.

> To this very day, I continue to own my first
> King James Bible and never travel without it.
> I also have the slip and can still wear it.

That night I ended up staying with Ms. Bert, after all.

Lora was a little girl on the 3rd floor that I played with occasionally. We'd not too long become friends. Lora had
plenty of dolls and her mother was warm. As I was walking
downstairs to take my things to Ms. Bert's apartment, Lora's
mother invited me to come to their party. She said in Africa
when a person passes on, they have a celebration and that's
what we would do. So they turned on the record player and
we danced to James Brown, 1972 style. I'd gotten lost in the
music and it did just what Lora's mother said — it took my
mind off of what had just happened, momentarily.

I looked up and Lora's mom said someone was there to see me.
For me? I wondered, '*who could this be?*' It was Vivas. He had
recently come back into Mama's life and was beginning to visit
us fairly often. I'd wondered if he'd also gotten the news, or was
it a planned visit? He had the look of devastation on his face and
asked me if it was true that Mama died that day. I said, "Yes, it is
true." Then he chastised me for dancing and carrying on. How
could I do such a thing as if nothing had occurred? Suddenly,
I was guilt-ridden for enjoying myself on such a sad day. I was
caught between two cultures.

> *Little did I know that would be the first of many occasions to come, where I would be the center of controversy over how I ought to be conducting myself, based on others' perceptions and cultural divisiveness.*

Mama told Vivas that I was his daughter, and I surmised that was why he'd been coming around being kind to us and bringing gifts. When he asked me what I wanted, I really didn't know. He told me kids my age had posters all over their room. I asked, "What were they for?" Sounded like a strange concept. When he brought the oversized poster we put it up on the wall. I liked the poster because it broke up the monotony of the empty wall, but the typewriter was the best gift. I taught myself how to type by learning the keys from the instructions in the box. That typewriter became the tool which allowed me to release the pain of my loss and was the catalyst for my future writings.

Vivas gave me $50 and we said our good-byes. I never saw or heard from him again. I used the money to purchase a new dress, gloves, purse and shoes for Mama's funeral.

That night I cried myself to sleep.

Nine years ago today
T'was a sunny, cold Sunday
The sun shone on the streets
Melting the icy snow
Oh but,
On the inside Darkness did reign
One's weakness controlled and
Death was victorious

I, but a child
Did not understand
The irony of it all until night fell.
And, nine years ago today
I cried myself to sleep
Yearning for one who would never return. [6]

---

6   February 26, 1981

The next morning I didn't go to school, because I was waiting for Uncle Raymond. I didn't know what time he would be there. I just knew he would be there. I stayed by the window most of the day, looking for his blue station wagon to pull up. He'd never been there before, but I knew he'd find me.

In my waiting and thinking, I realized my work was not done. I had goodbyes to take care of. Ms. Frances was back in her beauty shop. So, I went over go give her a hug and say goodbye.

> The summer before, Ms. Frances took me to her suburban home for a two-week vacation. It was the best vacation ever and I was treated royally! The reprieve from the ghetto showed me everyone in the ghetto is not of the ghetto. I loved her immaculate home with spacious kitchen, bright modern décor and airy windows. Of course, I did not want to leave and tried to devise ways to extend the holiday. However, Ms. Frances had to get back to work and the plan was to take me back at that time. After that, she and I remained very close. I would visit the shop and sit by her side as though she were Mahatma Gandhi.

While I was at her shop, I used the telephone to call Sister

Fisher. I'd memorized the number, HY 3-5414, in case I was ever in a jam. Particularly, to let her know where we'd moved to next. Mama would always ask, "How do those women know how to find us?" Between a precocious little girl, and the divine will of God, we were destined to remain bonded. After all, Sister Fisher and Sister Kemp were my appointed earthen angels.

When leaving Ms. Frances' shop, I walked back across the street and saw the Reverend of the Baptist Church on our block. Of course, he also heard and expressed condolences. What's more, he expressed a concern for me and conveyed a desire to adopt me into his family. After hearing this and knowing without a doubt I would have been in good, noble hands, I'd almost regretted my decision the day before.

Since we'd moved further away from Sister Fisher there were times I couldn't get to Dean Street for worship, so I'd visit churches on my block. For weeks I sat in the window, watching people dressed in white garbs go in and out of the Synagogue across the street. Finally, utter curiosity took over. I wanted to see what their worship experience was like, so one Sabbath I just walked on in. I absorbed all the essence of incense, candles and loving worship. Three buildings down from our apartment the sounds of the Baptist Church gospel choir beckoned me. The Baptist Church experience was quite different from the Synagogue and even Sister Fisher's Holiness Pentecostal Church, which also worshipped on the Sabbath. Trying not to be noticed, I'd quietly slip in and out. I went purely to have a personal experience with God, but I walked away with a greater reality. *I realized regardless of the denomination, God's spirit was present in each temple and as a child of God, I was welcome.*

When I'd said all my goodbyes and gotten back to Ms. Bert's apartment, I took my station in the window. While looking for Uncle Raymond's station wagon, I saw an entourage of children coming down the block. I looked and looked again. *Those are the girls from my 6th grade class.* I ran downstairs and they started talking before I could say a word. "Miss Mosely was concerned why you weren't in school today and asked if anyone knew why you were absent. Lela told her she'd heard your mother died. Miss Mosely wants to see you. So, she sent us to get you and take you back to school."

This was so amazing to me. The worst thing happened. Yet, I was receiving this outpouring of love. I certainly did not want to leave without seeing Miss Mosely. I loved Miss Mosely.

I admired Marilyn Mosely for her independent persona and exceptional beauty — she was a walking clone of Lola Folana, a very popular actress and dancer. Miss Mosely was firm and fair. She became my advocate when I went to her in tears because someone in the class had stolen an envelope stuffed full of change out of my pencil holder. I was accumulating the change for the church tithe. To keep Mama from confiscating the money, I placed it in my pencil holder inside my notebook. Mama's alcohol habit had gotten so out of control that she began snatching my church money. I broke down in tears because I was at my wits end, against all odds trying to do the right thing. There were no sacred places. Miss Mosely recovered the envelope without a dime missing.

Beyond all these wonderful characteristics, Miss Mosely had been paying attention where I was concerned. A few months into our term, a student was bumped up to our 6-1 class. Apparently, she'd far exceeded expectations for the 6-3 class. Miss Mosely asked me to *teach* — not tutor — teach the new student during lunch hours. My assignment was to catch the new student up on all the lessons she'd missed.

This special assignment made me blossom in ways I could not have imagined. First of all, it removed me from the crowd during lunch hours. Anything was liable to occur when all the kids gathered together in the schoolyard during and after school. I had often been in the middle of a lot of the skirmishes. *Just eliminating that bit of stress in my day worked wonders for my countenance.* Secondly, I learned I was more at ease in a one-on-one setting. Thirdly, we discovered that I had a great proficiency for conveying information. I used the chalkboard, administered and graded exercises, and patterned the same instruction sequence that I'd observed. The fact that I remembered the minute particulars entailed in all the previous lessons amazed me, but I didn't tell anyone.

I'd made a new friend, a close friend, a real friend. This new student became my best advocate. *I'd given her my best and in return she'd given me her friendship.* The experience gave me a special sense of accomplishment. I was chosen to do something that no one else could have done. I was the chosen student — teacher.

When we arrived at the school, the lunch period was over and class had already begun. So, Miss Mosely came outside the room to talk privately with me in the hall. I told her what had happened and that my uncle was coming to take me to North Carolina. She practically begged me to stay until the end of the school year, which would only be a few months away. Miss Mosely said I would be getting a lot of awards. *Despite all the troubles at home, I managed to get in all my lessons and remain in the top percentile of the class.* She even suggested I might have gotten the scholarship to Hunter College. No, the awards could not be sent to me. I had to finish the school year out.

As much as I wanted to see the rewards of a difficult, yet triumphant school year, Uncle Raymond was on his way and I would not be able to stay. We were both sad about that.

The walk back was bittersweet. I felt so alone. Strangely, I also felt a liberation I'd never known before. So much had occurred in a 24-hour span. Not only had I experienced the deterioration and passing of my mother, but I'd also touched death. I'd been double exposed on the rituals of death and felt associated guilt. I'd experienced an outpouring of love from adults and acceptance from my peers, which was something I'd been striving for all school year. I remember thinking, *'I finally get it and have to leave. Well, doesn't that beat all? As far as school goes, I can only imagine all the good things I'll be missing out on at graduation. But, at the same time, I'm hopeful good things await in North Carolina.'*

When I got back to Ms. Bert's apartment, Uncle Raymond had not yet arrived. I was not a bit worried, just anxious to see him. It wasn't long before the beautiful, blue station wagon pulled up. I saw it slowly coming up the street, and I was so happy! My knight in shining armor had come to my rescue. Not only was there Uncle Raymond, but Uncle Ruppert, Uncle Wayne and Butchie, Uncle Clarence's oldest son. We loaded up my bag of stuff. I got in the back and we were off.

Passing by my schoolyard, watching all the kids play felt odd. I was looking into the schoolyard from the other side of the fence. It was a surreal scene that represented an entire life I could now leave behind. I breathed a sigh of relief, but the memories left in Brooklyn would haunt my dreams for years to come.

Haunted Dreams

It took years for Brooklyn to get out of my system. Throughout my childhood, adolescence and into adulthood I would dream about those old gothic buildings. I'd run and hide. Seems as though each episode would become more and more intense. There was always a myriad of trap doors, one behind the other. I would escape into trap doors that no one knew was there, but me. I had secret escape routes, many of them, all on different floors; sometimes leading out of the building, sometimes not.

It was not a game. I was hiding to save my life. Once out of the building I ran and ran and ran, until my body released itself from my mind, forcing me to awaken out of the dream; lest I have a heart attack while in a subconscious state.

When I was small, Mama would be my safety reservoir after awakening from a bad dream. She'd always let me sleep under her and would wrap her big thigh all around my little body and only then would I feel safe. But Mama was gone now. The dreams did not go away, but lessened after an encounter with her one night. I was walking down a familiar street in Brooklyn. It looked like Quincy Street. I passed a building that my subconscious deemed as a place known to house elderly and insane persons. I had not seen Mama in a long time and something told me she was inside this treatment facility. I went inside and found her there. The room was very dark and dismal. An aged woman was in a rocking chair with her back turned three-quarters away from the room entrance. It was Mama. I could spot her anywhere. I couldn't discern, however, if she was in the facility because of old age or insanity.

I walked over to Mama and she didn't want to see me. In fact, she demanded that I leave her alone. I was so hurt. I pleaded with her, trying to understand, but she offered no explanations - just to go on and leave her alone.

The dream troubled me for months. Truthfully, it still does — now, thirty years later. I could not shake the dream and needed an interpretation. I trusted Uncle Raymond's wife, Aunt Mable. So I shared the dream with her and asked what it meant. Aunt Mable told me that Mama was saying to go on with my life and to let her go. It was so hard for me to let Mama go. As dysfunctional as her life became, I needed her. Only she knew what we had been through and I missed her so.

She never visited my dreams again, but I relived the emotion upon watching the movie, *What Dreams May Come.* In the movie Robin Williams' beautiful wife, played by Anabella Sciorra, commits suicide because she is overcome with grief over having lost her husband and children to a car accident. Their spirits have been transformed into the afterlife and he risks the spiritual journey to find her in the underworld with hopes of saving her. He finds her in the same dark, dismal place, in the same rocking chair, with the same charred spirit as I found Mama. This deja vu experience convinced me the human psyche is truly universal. Another human being experienced the same dream as I, and portrayed it in *What Dreams May Come.*

That wasn't the only foretelling dream I had as a youth. A year later, I dreamed Uncle Raymond was lying in a casket. The casket gleamed a sky blue metallic frame, lined in white satin, adorning my knight. He was the most handsome man in white I'd ever seen and looked like the picture of health. But, there he lied. I could not believe it. I awakened myself from the dream for a swift reality test. I made sure to see Uncle Raymond that day and couldn't help but to ask, "Uncle Raymond, do you feel OK?" He was fine. Thank God. "*I love you.*" Every opportunity from there on, I made sure to tell and show Uncle Raymond just how much I loved him.

> *Out of a fearful subconscious experience, I learned we must outwardly express our devotion to our loved ones while they are present to receive it.*

My dreams eventually evolved into great adventures of swimming large bodies of water or where I took on the ability to fly, most often over water. I flew with superhuman abilities, sometimes with a device, sometimes without. Swimming was calming and accomplishment oriented. Flying gave me a new freedom of mind and spirit never experienced in conscious state. *My subconscious was finally free from whatever I needed to be protected from. While in flight I navigated the course. Oh, what a feeling!*

ADVERSITY

Why should not some adversity befall you?
For it is what gives us our stripes
Our code of honor
Our courage
And fortitude.

Do not fear when adversity comes
Remember, the kite flies highest against the wind.
And so,
You will also fly
To meet your highest potential, because
Adversity honored you with the ability to overcome.

Sweet Transitions

I was glad to be in the South with its beautiful trees, grass and fresh air. The air was so fresh that you could smell rain before it arrived. It was a wonderful place for a child to experience growing up. The first year I lived with Grandma Kiter and Aunt Virginia. We called her *Big Mama*. She was big and everybody's Mama — the eldest sibling of nine Ferguson children. The best part was being reunited with old friends and cousins. What was even more exciting was that I had my first opportunity to engage in sports. Between the spring of my 6th grade year and 7th grade year I learned how to ride a bike, play basketball, swim and the art of cheerleading. I marveled at the grace and discipline of my friend Gloria and cousin Cheryl as cheerleaders. Cheryl was especially good at it. Therefore, I enlisted her as my trainer when I decided to try out for the junior high school squad.

Every day after school I'd go out on my grandmother's porch

and practice cheers by watching my reflection in her large picture window. This became a ritual — to the point where persons in the neighborhood would walk by and shout encouragements my way. However, Big Mama would say, "You're too stiff to be a cheerleader." Nonetheless, I kept practicing and discovered I was actually quite flexible. I enjoyed the accomplishment of watching progress in action. I could see my skills improving each week.

Finally, the day of tryouts came and I learned why they called it 'Tryouts.' Cause it was tryin'. Tryin' on your nerves, fa' sho! The winners would be announced at the year-end dance, the Sock Hop. Eight cheerleaders would be selected and they waited until the very end of the dance to announce the winners. Name after name was called, Gloria, Linda, Leigh, Shay, Julie, Elizabeth, Davia. Seven names had already been called. Disappointment settled in my chest and I was trying to hold it all in — lest I be accused of being a spoilsport. Then, I heard *my* name. I leaped a three-foot vertical into the air. That was a great lesson in perseverance.

Without realizing, I'd followed a process to attaining my goal. The sweetest thing about this accomplishment was that I had no previous knowledge about cheerleading. We didn't have sports in New York City elementary schools. Nonetheless, I set my mind to something I desired and by sheer determination it happened.

This lesson was one I could draw upon time and time again as the years went by: a) I set a goal; b) assessed my deficiencies; c) acquired the needed resources; d) applied the training provided via practice; e) followed a disciplined schedule; f) instituted reassessments via check point meetings with the trainer; g) was not deterred by those who did not support my goal; h) tried my best; i) proceeded in faith; and j) attained my goal.

Sometimes you'll make the mark, because the decision makers
will see your diligence and desire.
As I once heard, half of being successful is just showing up.
But, how you show up can be the difference maker.

Bitter Transitions

From external appearances it looked as though I was adjusting quite well. In addition to getting acclimated at school, I joined my cousins on the Junior Choir at St. Paul AME Zion Church where Aunt Jean was Minister of Music. However, internally many other things were going on. I missed Mama. I began writing scores of poetry to sooth my emptiness. The popular song *Have You Seen Her* by the Chi-Lites became my mantra. Dynamics in the Ferguson household changed after Grandma Kiter went to a nursing home and Big Mama lost her tenured employment with the prominent Broyhill family.

She'd been with Paul, Faye and their children, Caron, Claire and Hunt since the children were small. In fact, she practically nursed Hunt Broyhill. Big Mama prized those children and I suppose the status of having worked up close and personal with the stately family was most appealing, especially since many others in the community worked in Broyhill's furniture factories. However, the children were now of age and her services were no longer needed.

She resorted to accept a caretaker, cooking job in the evenings for another not-so prominent family. That left me home alone and every time the chauffeur drove her off for work, she'd say, "Now don't you go outside of the yard." *That didn't happen.* As soon as she drove off, I was gone somewhere. Up to the recreation center, down to Linda's house or up to Gloria's house. I just could not stay in the house or in the yard. The spirit of being on the move was imbedded in my limbs — more like my psyche.

Big Mama's expectation was likened to having an invisible canine fence. The dog could see beyond the yard space, but couldn't breach it. Well, that was not going to work. I loved the open spaces too much to be confined, especially in the spring of the year when all the children were out playing.

One of those afternoons, Big Mama shook her finger at me saying, "Don't leave the yard and I mean it!" As soon as the car was out of sight, I got on the big bike Uncle Raymond bought me and went flying down the hill on Arlington Circle. A car came around the circle and there wasn't enough room for the oncoming car, the one parked on the side of the road and me. So, I slowed down and moved over into a ditch until the car passed by. I must have hit a rock or something. The bike fell over and carried me along with it. Somehow I managed out of the ditch and started walking over to Linda's house. When I looked down to see if my knee was scraped up, I just about went into shock. The skin beneath the kneecap was completely torn from the bone. With bone exposed and blood dripping down my leg - likened to a war soldier, I felt no pain and kept walking toward my friend's house. Linda's mother rushed me to the emergency room and when I arrived, there was my knight in shining armor, Uncle Raymond. *How did he know?* Even though I was wrong for disobeying, he didn't scold me about it. He was more concerned about my well-being. Dr. Phillip Fail, the Ferguson family doctor, stitched me up and sent me home.

I became impatient after the first month of lying around with salt pad soaks. The dog days of summer were dragging like thick molasses. All my friends were going to the pool. I could walk and had the fever for swimming, so I found a way to sneak off to the West End pool. Everyone was at the pool. Unbeknownst to me, the chlorine in the pool aided my healing exponentially. The wound closed up and began its own natural healing process. Afterwards I began to test the waters, but in other ways. Sneaking off became more of a sport to see how often I could go off and get back before Big Mama arrived.

I usually spent evenings with the DeVanes. Heretofore, they were the most *normal* family I had the privilege to be a part of. Gloria DeVane was one of my best friends. She had an older sister, an older brother, a sweet mother who was one of my teachers and a quiet father who was well respected in the community as Assistant Superintendent of Schools. They all lived contentedly under the same roof. Their brick home was immaculate, surrounded by a big yard that overlooked the local junior high school ball field. The view from the field yielded a panoramic view of Grandfather Mountain, nestled in the Appalachian Blue Ridge Mountains. I marveled when someone pointed out nature's carving of its grandfather image. If you can imagine, there was plenty of green space in view. In the fall, Gloria and I helped her father rake leaves. After all the leaves were bound together in two large piles, we would take running jumps into the mounds — face forward. That was freedom!

But, all good things must come to an end. One day I tested Big Mama a bit too far and she set out to whip me. I hated those little switches, 'cause they stung like fire. But, this time she got a branch and swapped that thing across my mid-section. By the sound of my scream, you would have thought a bus had hit me. I ran up to the DeVanes and called Uncle Raymond to come get me. When he saw the huge welt still on my stomach, he decided it was time to move me. I wanted to live with him all along and that was my true motivation. I loved my uncle more than anyone in the whole world. Plus, his wife was generous with her time, kindness and wisdom. To live with them was my heart's desire.

Just when I was getting comfortably settled at Uncle Raymond's, I was told I would be moving with Aunt Mable's daughter. I'd spent some time with her and her two children at family dinners and a few outings, and knew them as cousins through marriage. I even called Aunt Mable's daughter by her first name, which established a friendship basis according to the way I'd been taught. However, as soon as I moved into the household the entire relationship chart changed. Instead of being a cousin, I was now sister to two younger brothers and had a new mother. I'd never been a sister to anyone and my mother had just died. Yet, I was expected to understand these roles and fall in line. There was no adjustment period and little room for error. Even though I was finally placed in a stable household and in time acclimated to the family order, the following five years were full of turmoil and misunderstanding.

Despite my willful adolescent struggles, I was ever mindful that the wrong move might land me into the foster care system. Therefore, I bided time until my eighteenth birthday.

SECRET PLACE

When I was a child
I'd go to a secret place
Where no one else would be.
A place where I could find myself
And all sorts of discoveries.
In my special place there was
Sand and a stream
A place where I was free to dream
Of how my life would be.

One with nature,
I was in peace
During my time at the Beach.
That's what I call my special place
No one knew where it was
I'd dare not share
For if I did,
Its solitude would lose its trace.

Pay It Forward

When my senior year of high school approached, I took the SAT test, applied to colleges, and was accepted to several state universities. For the benefit of my future, I did something unprecedented. I mustered the courage to walk into my high school Guidance Counselor's office and shed my familial secrets. I told Mrs. Franklin about my quandary. There was no money set aside for my education. I needed her assistance to obtain financing, or else I would not be able to attend college, despite the fact that I'd already been accepted. During my junior year at Lenoir High School, I was a National Honor Society student. Lenoir High closed and in my senior year we merged into a brand new school, West Caldwell High. Among West Caldwell's first graduating class, I ranked number seventeen and was a Beta Club honor student.

At graduation I also received the top GPA medal within the

Home Economics department, as a result of a Family Life Education course taken my senior year. *What irony!* Even though stable family life eluded me, the award demonstrated I had an advanced understanding of the psychological dynamics of family life.

Mrs. Franklin provided instruction on the Pell grant application process and researched scholarships for which I was eligible. She was President of the Caldwell County Business and Professional Women's Club and recommended me for the organization's continuing education scholarship. I was also recommended for the James G. K. McClure Foundation Scholarship, based in Asheville, North Carolina. I was required to write an extensive paper describing why I was worthy of the scholarship. In secluded, private moments, I drafted the letter and left out no significant elements. I had the grades, the desire, an impoverished legacy starting out of the blocks, no money, and no commitments of future support.

If it was to be, it was up to me.

I was awarded both scholarships and maximum financial aid to begin my first year at the University of North Carolina at Greensboro. *So even though I missed the scholarship to Hunter College, God had another blessing in store for me.*

As an independent student I was blessed with four years of

full financial aid, which included on-campus work in the Sociology Department and The Center for Applied Research within the Bryan School of Business.

At The Center for Applied Research I acquired a wonderful advocate in Dr. Donald Judd, who was the Director of the Center and Chair of the Economics Department. In addition to my normal duties as his research assistant, Dr. Judd looked out for me via additional work opportunities. Through his recommendation, I worked as a research canvasser for an Alcoholic Drinking Habits Study conducted by the Center for Disease Control. Of course, you know I had an interest in the outcome of this study and if I could play a role to bring awareness on the affects of alcohol, I was more than pleased to walk the blocks, knock on doors, gather information, leave tracking and incentive sheets and pray that the participants were honest in their recordings.

The Center had *"a"* cutting edge word processor, a PC predecessor, and I was one of a privileged few with access to *it*. Having access to the word processor was like having top-secret security clearance. As a result of becoming proficient with the technology, Dr. Judd recommended my skills to his authoring colleagues. He allowed me key access to the Center after hours and on weekends to enable my extra work. *Who would have ever thought we were laying the foundation for my future endeavors?*

> *I honestly can say, I do not know where I would be in life or what road I would have taken without this advanced educational opportunity.*

I thank God everyday for this blessing, for it has greatly impacted my life. I promised God I would publicly thank Him for providing my college education and for putting Sue Franklin in my path. I also promised I would be an instrument to help other worthy students, who do not have the financial means to pay for college. I am grateful both have come to pass.

April 15th

April 15, 1992 seemed like most any other work-
day. I'd already completed my tax returns, so I didn't have
that pressure hanging over my head. I held a high-energy
managerial position with a leading Fortune 500 corporation
and with the overload task of balancing people and project
responsibilities, I took my role seriously. During this time,
I was in the throes of collaborating with IT programmers,
developing new business systems for my business unit, evaluating company policy and protocols, developing procedural
manuals, addressing employee performance reviews and
completing certification as a Quality Administrator, among
an abundance of other managerial duties.

I enjoyed leveraging teams and applying a systemic process
toward obtaining positive results. I didn't realize it at the
time, but I suppose because so much in my past had been out
of my control, any system that could create order and yield

positive results was something I was naturally drawn to. I absorbed the concepts like milk to a baby. I applied the concepts like a child discovering its toes were useful for walking. The rewards were bountiful and seemed endless. I was beginning a successful career phase.

I remember the day as if it were yesterday. Around mid-afternoon, I routinely checked my mailbox. There were several inter-office memos, and Home Office procedural protocols — or General Bulletins. I was the type of manager that read every single memo, General Bulletin, etc. I wanted to be informed and took every precaution not to be caught off guard or uninformed about my area of responsibility. In order to stay on top of information, my habit was to go off site several times a week during the quiet of an uninterrupted lunch and read 'route,' as we called it.

Amidst the bundle of mail, there was an inter-office envelope from Human Resources. Not unusual. I thought some typical correspondence relating to one of my employees. What I found inside the envelope was anything but typical, nor was it related to any of my employees. There were several confidential documents inside this inconspicuous envelope, all relating to *me*. The trail of documents started with a form memo from the Salvation Army's Missing Persons division. Within the form memo, my name was inserted as the "missing person" at last known address, "7xx Quincy Street,

Brooklyn, New York . . . a relative desires to hear from you."

Missing person? I am a missing person?"

The letter had been sent to the Social Security Administration. You'd guess! They indexed their system to locate my social security number. Once that was determined, it was not difficult to find my employer of record. My blood pressure jumped a meter when I saw the document had been forwarded to my company's Home Office. That was bad enough, but it was then sent to the local human resource office in Charlotte, North Carolina. No doubt, after having gone through several hands locally, the information was eventually addressed to me. I was in a semi state of shock. There was a disclaimer on the memo, stating I did not have to respond to the inquiry, but if I wished to a number was listed. I wanted to delay the call, but my curiosity was on high edge. So I called. The number was from the originating source, The Salvation Army. The person on the other end of the telephone was calming and informed, "Your brother is anxious to find you." I had no idea I had a lost brother. No . . . *apparently I was the one who was lost.*

I then took the liberty to use my manager's office, closed the door and made the call. It never occurred to me that I was infringing upon his private space or that I was being unethical by placing a personal, long distance call. This was of the utmost importance and had to be handled right then. I dialed the 718 area code — New York. I've run from it all my life and now I am circling right back to New York. My gut told me there was truth in the letter. "Hello," the telephone was answered and Pandora became unleashed. Not only did I have a brother, but two brothers and two sisters. One of the brothers was a year younger than I. They were scattered all over the United States and had been separated for many, many years. He confirmed the birth mother's name.

Oh my God, she's real. There is a person named Emily Crotti. I'd convinced myself, Emily Crotti was one of Mama's aliases.

What's more, this mother was alive. There was more. So much more, that I became overloaded.

The door opened and my manager gave me the look of, "What are you doing in MY office." That was my cue. I needed to break away from the call to process all I'd just heard.

What do I do now?

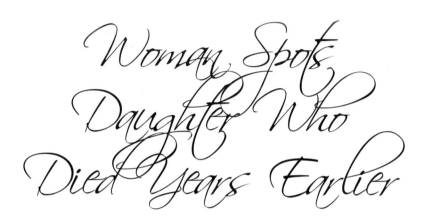

Woman Spots Daughter Who Died Years Earlier

How can you reconcile thirty-two gaping, missing-in-action years within a six-hour time frame? Yet, this is what I went to do, traversing as far across the United States as I could possibly go. I went with deep-seated trepidation, overshadowed by hopefulness and courage. Remembering the Serenity Prayer tucked away in the crevices of my soul ... *'God grant me the serenity to accept the things I cannot change. The courage to change the things I can; and the wisdom to know the difference.'*

Aunt Mable gave me this modestly framed prayer when I

was a teenager. I carried the prayer with me to college and the prayer remained prominently displayed as one of my prized possessions for many years going forward. When Uncle Raymond passed away in 1988, I recycled the frame to hold an endearing photo of my knight in shining armor. But the prayer was discarded, because I thought I'd outgrown it. Besides the words were forever imprinted in my mind and spirit. When the Serenity Prayer was given to me, I did not have the breadth of knowledge to understand its true connection to my life. Nor did I understand how important such a prayer would be for my future peace of mind.

As worldly and street smart as I thought I was, there remained a tender nuance of trust and naiveté that I was constantly taken to task on as an adolescent. "You are so naive, and too trusting of your friends." For me, close friends were family and no amount of confusion could break our bond. We pierced our fingers to share the kinship of being blood-sisters, bound by our word. Yet, I'd foolishly gone into relationships time and time again with the expectation of loyalty among misguided kindred spirits.

So, once again I put myself on the risk-laden tightrope . . . out on a limb to seek the love that had been missing for thirty-two years . . . my entire life. I went seeking the answers to my longing desire to bond with one that could surely love me unconditionally, because she created me within her womb. One who once nurtured me upon her breast and protected me for the first days and months of my existence into the world. Yet, I recalled being forewarned, "She was not happy you've been found."

I'd entrusted my discovery to a long term confidant and asked if he would accompany me on this vital journey. We landed in San Francisco and spent the night. There was no conversation of the day to follow. By external appearances, it all looked like two happy go lucky people vacationing to embark upon new territory. And all new territory it would be. The next morning we began our trek to Merced, enjoying the view of miles upon miles of rolling hills distinguished by row upon row of windmill generators. I became engrossed in the nuance of the environment. Until ... my first pang of anxiety hit when I saw the mileage sign, Merced — 20 miles. *"We're close."* My heart began to race. Upon entering the small town, my chest began to swell and breathing was rapid. We carefully followed directions as to not get lost. In a blink of an eye we were in a modest subdivision, and there was the sign — Stratford Avenue. I began to tremble with uncontrollable fear, experiencing my *first full-blown anxiety attack.* I could not breathe. My heart was tight and I thought I would nearly have a heart attack. I'd traveled so far, but wanted to go back.

"Stop the car ... I cannot do it ... I cannot do it ... Let's go back ... Please take me back ... I cannot do it."

Tears were rolling down my face like drenched ice droplets in a hailstorm. They ran hard, fast and uncontrollably. For the first time in my *adult* life I felt *completely* vulnerable and powerless. I felt like a sheep that had wandered too far from home, and moaned to be rescued. With a quivered voice I begged, "*Take me back. I cannot do this.*" But, we'd come too far. No pain, no gain. The risk had to be worth it. You never know unless you try. My companion encouraged me and patiently insisted I calm down. "You CAN do this. You NEED to do this." We circled the area three times before I was able to calm myself down. Yet, my hands remained trembling.

He gets out of the car to approach the door and rings the bell.

Oh, my God. There she is.

He comes to get me out of the car and graciously escorts me to my mother — this time my *real* mother. How do I know for sure? I've been lied to so often through the years. How will I know absolute truth when I see it? Yet, it stared me back in my face — a mirror image of my person. Astonishing!

I see a woman looking at me who is my twin. She bears the same height, the same frame, the same face, the same hands, the same fingers, same everything.

I approach in silence. She approaches in silence. We reach out to hug. I hang on a bit to test my emotions. I feel nothing. This is my first disappointment.

We enter the house and I meet her husband, who happens to be African American and from known accounts her third husband. "Yeah, you sure do look like your mother. There's no mistaking on that. You are her daughter. You know, a long time ago she told me she had another daughter, but she said — well, she said — the child died."

I am floored at this point. Eyes wide as saucers and mouth wide open. Dropping my head into my hands, I weep. This is how I've been explained away all these years. I do not exist in her mind. She went back for all her other children, but I was pronounced DEAD. I was ready to go. Leaning against my strong companion, "*I can't handle this. It's too much for me.*"

"No, stay now. It will be OK," he consoled.

Her husband walks out of the room, mumbling. I quickly surmise he is an ignorant *so and so*. In such a delicate situation, how can you in any reasonable mind set tell a young woman to her face upon meeting her mother, for the first time in memory, that she has been considered dead her entire life? Since he had to be present, I would just ignore him for the remainder of the visit and focus on the person I came to see. I had a million and one questions, and she is the only person who knows the answers, the right answers, and the truth.

Ye shall know the truth and the truth shall set you free.[7]

My soul screams,

I WANT TO BE FREE!

Let the dance begin. The dance of denial. The dance of facade. The dance of shame and deception. The dance of forgiveness. She entertains me as though I were a long-time friend with whom she hasn't communed in a while. You know how we do.

"Sit down. Can I get you anything? How was your trip? Have you been to California before? I am preparing dinner, would you like to eat?"

If pop ups were visible!

EAT? Who cares about food at a time like this?
EAT? Who can eat at a time like this?
I don't give a **** about food.
Do you think I came all this way to eat a meal?
I could have eaten at any restaurant along the way.

---

7   John 8:32

But no, I cannot say those things.

My reply is, "*Whatever you prepare will be fine.*" Then she asks, "What is your favorite food?"

> *I can't even think right now, and you want me to think about my favorite food. This is surreal. Tell me I am dreaming.*

"*I don't have a favorite food.*" I dare not let on Italian spaghetti is my all time favorite, make-me-happy dish.

"Well, I thought I'd prepare spaghetti. Do you like spaghetti"?

OK, that figures. Trying to appear indifferent I say, "*Yes, I like spaghetti.*"

In keeping with the facade, the dance, the play of all plays, she asks if I would like to help her in the kitchen. I think, '*If this is what it will take to get close to you, of course I will help prepare the meal. I am in the lion's den now. I am here for a purpose and to leave without fulfilling my mission would devastate me. I will do most anything she would ask of me for the time I am here.*'

While I carefully watch her cut fresh Italian sausage and all the ingredients that I also use in my spaghetti dish, I begin

119

to carefully select my arsenal of questions. What can I start with that is least challenging? OK, here goes —

"*What happened that day?*"

"That day?"

"*Yes, the day you gave me up. How did that come about?*"

"Well, sweetie — I didn't give you up. Your father gave you to your mother that raised you. You know they had a thing and he took you to her."

"*Why would he do such a thing?*" "*Where were you?*"

She could not account for her whereabouts, or his motivations, nor her role in any circumstances leading up to THAT DAY. It was the fault of everyone else, but she was blameless. She was kicked out of the house at an early age, a victim of incest, she says. "I was treated like the black sheep of the family."

Was it because she inherited a darker complexion and had thick, curly, nearly kinky hair?

She tells me it was because she believed in 'diversity.'

120

It was the 60s, and she was part of a new generation, those who experimented with inclusiveness, the togetherness movement. They desired freedom from social injustice and parental bondage.

At age eleven her father, Peter Crotti, voyaged to the United States from Dorno, Italy. His father, Giovanni Antonio Crotti, made several trips to the USA in the early 1900s to seek opportunity for his family. Giovanni, his uncles and other relatives worked on the construction of tunnels and bridges that connect NYC to its boroughs. I am told his son, my grandfather, made his livelihood working on the docks in New Jersey, a common path for many Italian immigrants. Emily's maternal grandparents, Bernardo Giarraputo and Calagera Belillo took the voyage from Santa Margarita, Sicily to America in 1902 and 1905, respectively. Bernardo owned a successful custom tailoring business that afforded the family a summer home in Long Island. They had seven children, all of whom prospered well, some more than others. The second oldest was Rose, my grandmother. The family's philosophy was to mix and mingle with your own kind, but Emily wanted to explore.

"I was twenty-one years old having to struggle with four children and another one on the way. You were the baby."

I was the *baby*. An innocent, helpless baby — whose mother abandoned her and has no explanation, rhyme or reason for her action. *I deserve to know the TRUTH. The gory, forbidden, shameful truth — however it may be. Just please tell me the truth and leave nothing to my imagination.*

But no, she did not give me the truth. It was as though she did not know the truth herself. She'd told so many lies, for so many years. She had to mask the truth in order to survive emotionally. She convinced herself, her husband and her other children that one of her children no longer existed. "I once had another daughter, but she died." "You had a twin sister, but she died."

How cruel to tell a child there was another human being who shared her life beginnings, but the twin did not make the journey. My sister yearned for this twin she was told about, but never got to know. Ironically, we looked so much alike as babies I found her picture and was told it was mine. The Polaroid pre-dated my birth. As an elementary age child, I was astute enough to know that was impossible. I gave it away in an elementary school baby-picture swap. It was the only baby picture we had, now gone. Unbeknownst to me, this black and white photo of a bouncy baby girl was a beautiful picture of Doris, my sibling one year older.

She went on, "Women in the 60s didn't have opportunities like they do today. There weren't programs like there are today to help women. I had no education. I had to do whatever I could. I left my children with my mother for a time to go figure out some way to make money. My husband, Frank, your father, was in jail at the time. He was no help."

I think, '*was Frank really my father, or is that what you must say to save face?'*

"When I came back, I found out my mother had called Social Services to pick up my children, saying she couldn't take care of them."

> The three older toddlers were in the care of their grandparents. The history behind who, when, where and more so 'why' I was given to someone outside the family *remains a mystery.*

"You must have been gone a long time, for her to do something like that."

"I told her I was coming back. It's my mother's fault and Frank's fault. I was only twenty-one, with four children and pregnant again. I did the best I could."

"I understand that you knew Irene, or Pat. Did you know her

real name was Irene?" Yes, she knew. That told me a lot right there. The average person did not know Mama's real name was Irene. They had to have been close.

"I understand there are letters where your mother attempted to reach her, asking to bring me by so she could see her granddaughter; and if she'd taken me to the doctor for (immunization) shots." But, the letters were returned, undeliverable. Eventually, the letters stopped.

> All those years we kept moving I thought it was because we were attempting to upgrade our living status. The fact is, Mama loved me *so much* she didn't want anyone to take me from her. I was the only positive thing in her life. She'd often say, "If something were to happen to you, I would have no reason to live." That statement put a heavy burden of responsibility on me. I had to be extra careful.

I found it interesting that there was a connection between Mama and my Grandmother, as my Aunt Lillian later shared her recollection of the story. "Pat was a nice lady. We knew you were with her."

> They all knew I was in the care of a high yellow, racially mixed Black woman who passed for Puerto Rican under the name of Pat Ortiz

Vivas. Both of Mama's parents were interracial several generations back, as products of a slave-master union. I saw photographs of Mama's grandmother, Julia, a slender woman with milky-cream skin. Her daughter, Grandma Kiter, took on the genetic traits from her father's Cherokee Indian bloodline. She had the most radiant black hair and a beautiful yellow-bronze complexion. When she became an aged woman, her skin thinned and you could see her strong veins running vibrantly throughout her frame. I have vivid memories of watching her brush her long black strands several times a day. At 80 years old she had very little gray.

Mama's father, Papa Jess, was also a man of high complexion and chiseled features. He'd already passed away by the time I was brought into the Ferguson family. Nonetheless, his photographs and legacy demonstrated a strong, handsome, well-respected man. Mama inherited a physical beauty from both, but clearly her mixed Cherokee Indian traits were the ones that enabled her to pass for Hispanic. [8]

---

8 Conclusion is based upon having spent time in Cherokee, NC. I saw my mother's features in many of the tribe's members.

"So, you also knew Mama? How did you know her?"

"She was tough. You wouldn't want to cross her."

> Mama was tough, 'cause she had to be. In her world, *"only the strong survived"* — her credo. However, her will broke under the hand of domestic violence and I watched her strong wall shatter bit by bit.

"I was younger, but the three of us, would steal checks out of mailboxes and cash them." I think, *'old habits are hard to break.'*

> In the lean days, Mama would take me with her to the Central Post Office the first of the month to intercept delivery of our welfare check. In those days, our address changed so often the mailman could not keep up with us and I guess she wanted DSS to think we still lived at our old address, so they wouldn't investigate. At that time, we were staying with an old lady, who was in her last days. Mama would pick up her check too. But, when the old lady passed away, we continued living in her apartment and the checks kept coming. Apparently, no one notified Social Services that the wom-

an had passed away. We would go to a neighborhood clear across Bed-Stuy every month in order to cash this check. Mama would always tell me to stay close, "—because in that neighborhood there were plenty of Gypsies, and the Gypsies steal children."

It used to blow me away how Mama routinely was able to pull this off without having to produce identification. I was her sidekick. Surely a woman with such a darling little girl would not be a thief. That is what people call folk who forge checks, right? I was bright enough to realize this was better than a lesser alternative. Besides, it kept a roof over our heads until Mama could figure out a better solution to our financial woes.

She continues, "I knew you'd moved down South after Pat died, but I thought it was best to leave you where you were."

She knew where I was all along. The game was over. She was always one up on me. She had knowledge. I did not. No matter how I spun the questions, she was a locked box. Pandora was not coming out to play today. My efforts were futile. I was about to leave empty handed.

But no, before I go let me touch her hair *now* while she's sitting and I stand close enough to touch her. This may be my only vantage point, *ever*. Running my fingers into her head of beautiful silken thick, textured locks of red and brown hue, if feels so familiar. Something converged between us. Comforting only for a few fleeting moments. Time stood still while I recaptured my bond reminiscent. Let me not be intrusive. I already have. She's obviously run out of small talk. My time is up.

Twelve years later (2004), I read the news headline: "Woman Spots Daughter who Died Years Earlier." I thought, '*I could write that story better than anyone else.*

It is my story.'

Choose You This Day

As much as I desired the truth and sought to embrace it, I found myself in stages of anger, denial, shame and
even confusion at times. Not understanding all these phases
represented stages of loss. What I'd lost was a sense of identity. This newfound truth confirmed I was, in fact, not Irene
Ferguson's child. Nor was I biologically akin to Uncle Raymond or the rest of the Ferguson family. It was amidst this
family that I found my first sense of belonging. That belief
justified my battles as a child, having to fight for my space
in the Black community. To finally accept that it was all a
charade angered me to no degree. Why did I go through
. . . watching Mama die . . . carrying the burden of her death
. . . life in the ghetto . . . the name calling . . . the gossip . . .
the racial snickers and stammers . . . the "whose child," and
endless "what are you" questioning? Do you mean to tell me

that this was never intended to be my birthright or wrong, whichever way we choose to look at it?

I felt deceived. To better understand the psychological impact, I purchased a book entitled, *The Dance of Deception*. To this day, I have not been able to read the book. My anger was exacerbated with thoughts that the challenges I've faced were a direct result of two irresponsible parents . . . two people that I never knew.

> *Of course, it has since occurred to me that my path was predetermined. Just as a manager used to commonly say, "You're just the man for the job," I think in eternity some are chosen for a special assignment that no one else can justly fulfill.*

Prior to accepting this realization, I put the burden of blame on my birth mother, lambasting her for abandoning her children and giving me away. As time went on and I later experienced becoming a mother, I reached out for her. However, this was subsequent to losing my baby after a long, excruciating and life threatening premature delivery. I was weak from battle and stripped of all coping mechanisms. With this child I would finally have my own family. The career switch was turned off and the mommy switch was on. Bone of my bone. Flesh of my flesh. All my hopes and dreams were gone. A major part of me died. I yearned for the comfort of a mother. I reached out to the mother who reared me during adolescence, but the only consolation she offered was to say, "You're not the only person who's ever lost a baby." Those words cut deeply and that place has not mended since. Then, I thought about Mama and I associated a time when we were inseparable, when I felt protected and loved and fantasized about how she would comfort me, *if only she were here.* Then another thought raced to mind, *I do have a mother and she's alive. She brought me into the world. Surely, she'll understand what I am going through.*

Yes, she did understand what I'd been through. She had also lost a baby boy at age 37 and experienced a long, excruciating premature labor bringing me into the world. I thought this dialogue would spawn an open door to address my unanswered questions. Although I didn't get the answers I sought, those short-lived conversations and subsequent letters reflected a bigger picture. There were many influential dynamics enveloping the situation of my birth and separation that involved familial and cultural norms, economics, marital discord, and many more complicated issues that may forever remain a mystery.

Nonetheless ...

The real world continued. I still had managerial duties. Who would give me a pass to slack off because I was having a crisis? I would put on my iron gird to bind up my pain and bury myself in work for another eight to ten hours. Afterwards I could get back home where I was glad to be living alone, so I could privately release my pain. I sent cries to God — *Why? Why? Why?*

Have you ever sent a wail out to the Lord?
Such a loud cry that you could hear
The sound waves echo
Throughout the universe.

God heard your wail
And sent His angels to reply

They came to lift your burden
Angels came 'cause you were hurting

I know you sent a wailing
I can see the stain marked in your eyes

I looked into them
And saw a reflection of mine[9]

---

9 Excerpt from Metamorphosis: A Life Journey, 1996

In the midst, I was once again caught between the expectation of who others thought I was and who they thought I ought to be. And not just that, but who I ought to be with.

My brother who so lovingly searched me out was now dictating, "Now that you know the truth, you should leave those people alone. Come on over to the right side." When I didn't comply he chastised that I was "*living a lie*" by continuing to live as I'd always been — as racially mixed, embracing my African American community.

Conversely, at the same time that all of this was going on, a childhood friend resurfaced. We'd been estranged for many years, after having gone separate paths post high school. Apparently, she held a great deal of animosity toward me, suggesting I'd discarded the friendship. I was deluged with attacking letters that read such things as being a *sellout*, because I was chasing the corporate ladder pretending to be White.

> Some people will never get that success is a product of consistent work ethic and quality results. *For instance*, I've witnessed critics saying, If you're Black and get promoted it was because of affirmative action, or because the individual Uncle Tom'd his way to the top. In some cases the latter is true, but most often than not, stripes are earned.

In this case, I was literally being compared to the girl in *Imitation of Life*, who denied even her mother to seek a life that would only be afforded to her, if she *passed*.

My desire was to uphold integrity and self-preservation, being true to myself and to those closest to me. I did not want to continue to perpetrate the deceit that was proffered to me. Yet, I could not undo thirty-two years of conditioning.

In my confusion, I contacted one of my dearest friends who'd given me the honor of being her first child's godmother. We discussed the seriousness of the role, not just the title. For this reason I thought it best she know that I'd found out my birth mother was in fact, Italian, not Black. Therefore, that meant I was Italian. Did she still want me to be godmother of her precious little girl?

My friend was the first to reassure me that this revelation had no bearing, whatsoever, on my role as her child's godmother, nor our friendship. This had been solidified years ago. My faithfulness as a friend was true blue — if color needed to be a part of the equation. Joyce wanted to send our tale of friendship to a magazine. This was a time when diversity issues were just beginning to get serious attention and she felt the article would be accepted. But, I begged her not. I wasn't ready to be exposed, nor was I prepared for the critics. I was still under the *"what will people say?"* cloud.

Then I turned to God, *"God, who do you say I am? What should I say I am?"*

God answered,
"It does not matter the medium in which you entered the world. You are my child."

From that moment on, I began to unravel my identity separate and apart from color boundaries. I certainly cannot deny the culture that is so ingrained in my thought processes, rhythm and ethos preference. Nor do I want to deny the genetics bound within my (maternal) DNA. Yet, I am woefully aware that it is only one half of the DNA story.

I've carried the name of a man whom I cannot identify and by all factual accounts is no longer living.[10] There is no known evidence to bear proof his seed created me, just a name on a birth certificate. Yet, throughout life I have consistently been baffled to answer and own up to the heritage behind his name. I think I have finally mastered the eloquence of saying, "I do not know."

---

10 Frank V. Schulz died in 1972 at age 40. No one knows the circumstances of his early death, except some say of a broken heart aided by alcoholism for having lost his family. He served the United States military as a sheet metal specialist. There were no taps played at his funeral. There was no flag or even mourners present to honor his life. He was buried in Potter's Field, a cemetery for the indigent.

Despite whatever remains missing, I have much to be proud of. Moreover, the shame I once masked has since been annulled by the grace of God.

The Healing Balm

It's taken me thirteen to thirty years, depending on when one chooses to start the clock, to grasp the reality that I was an abandoned infant, reared in false pretense regarding my parentage and origin, that I'll never know my natural father and that I missed out on the privilege of a stable childhood. I grew up with the mind set that one should not air one's dirty laundry and this was as dirty as it comes. So, I folded each piece of my laundry and neatly put it away into an obscure place where no one could find it.

When I turned eighteen and was released to the world, I was determined to shed my past. I would not allow my childhood experiences to determine or limit my future. For a time, I was successful at controlling the outcomes. I was able to obtain a college education and put it to use in the ranks of corporate America via roles that fed my need for belonging and accomplishment. I reaped the financial rewards of hard work invested with good salaries, fast promotions, bonuses and special assignments. Yet, as hard as I tried to inhibit my past through my accomplishments, I found myself going through intermittent periods of despair, particularly after all the accolades faded, were forgotten and accounted for nothing. I began asking myself why does *this* keep coming back. Yet, I could not define *this*. It was indicative of the recurring nightmares of my youth and early adulthood.

It was not until I experienced the process of becoming a mother, having grown attached to the life developing inside of me that I began to feel a correlation to my own development while in my birth mother's womb. That uncanny sensory memory kicked in and I felt a maternal connection to my biological source. Having also been enticed by the empirical notion of my medical doctor that I "have a survival gene." I longed to know the source of this genetic code and then began a quest to piece the puzzle together.

The puzzle is an intricate design
woven of spiritual, genetic, historical
and experiential pieces, some yet to be discovered.

Instead of continuing to bury my past, now I examine myself on a continuum seeking to understand and *accept* how the past has formulated my personality with all its intricacies that make me a unique human being, whom I've grown to appreciate and love.

I can love me, because I have comfort in knowing Jesus loves me. It's not just a song. It is a spiritual truth revealed. He revealed it to me in an extraordinary way. For this love to become a reality in your life, you must seek a relationship with the Lord for yourself.

I can love me, because I have comfort in knowing the Father has and will provide for me. I can love me, because I can walk in assurance that the Father has and will protect me from hurt, harm and dangers.[11]

I can love me, because I can lift my head in confidence knowing the Holy Spirit equips me with faithful insight to take whatever comes my way and somehow *squeeze out* some goodness. *For all things work for good, for those who love the Lord and are called to His purpose.*[12]

I can love me because God revealed, "It does not matter the medium in which you entered into the world. You are MY child." That confirms for me an intuitive truth I've always known. *I am a spiritual being having a human experience. It's all a test. To pass you must endure the world, yet not become consumed by the world. Your spiritual reward will be to enter into eternal life with the Father and the Son, our Savior Jesus Christ.*

---

11 Proverbs 1:33

12 Romans 8:28

In the meantime, we can persevere to make the best of whatever this life brings. Whether it means having to endure difficult circumstances that were inherited, cast upon us, or those created by our own decisions, life can still be joyful. My hope remains that this story will instill within you a "can-do" spirit. I want you to feel with total conviction and affirm with your mouth, "If she can come through all of that restored, sane and purposeful, surely I can!" *Through God's grace, we can.* Sit back in comfort and faith, knowing that as a child of the universe, God has your back. And don't forget —

Savor each and every drop of that sweet lemonade.

I can do all things

through Christ

who strengthens me.

— *Philippians 4:13*

Epilogue

First and foremost, God's purpose for this book is that it be used as an instrument for healing and to proclaim the truth that only through Him can we be healed. He calls out to lay it all on the altar and let Him be your resting place. He wants His children liberated from the world. God wants you to know peace beyond all understanding. Clearly, God's hands of mercy and protection have been upon my life. Just as the Psalmist David, I have a heart of thanksgiving. I am humbled to be chosen for this life and to be instilled with the courage to share it with you, so that you will also be inspired to seek Him.

My personal concern is for children living in the shadows of society. They are there, but you do not see what trails behind them as they travel forward. They trail in shadows left by their parents. Responsible parents recognize the impact of their influence and most people I know are truly the best at caring for and protecting their children. However, I remember every detail of my childhood and whereas some would think I was given a new start as an adolescent, I still carried my childhood with me. There was an entire history trapped inside me.

I need to be clear that social maladies *do not* go unnoticed in a child's psyche. They are manifested in ways the child will not recognize, even into adulthood. Witnessing violence, especially when it occurs in the place that is supposed to be the safest of all — a place called home, indelibly impacts children. Being homeless is something you never forget, no matter how hard you may try. I thank God every day for my humble home. Despite any financial upheavals I've experienced, God has always seen fit to maintain a house that is mine to call home. Losing a parent to death, prison, addictions or emotional abandonment is devastating for any child of any age and leaves scars. Scars of the worse kind, the ones we cannot see.

My pastor sermoned on how the Virgin Mary must have struggled with the legitimacy issue in her community. Being an expectant mother, out of wedlock, during such a traditional time, Mary was probably ridiculed. Who other than her, Joseph, the Wise Men and Elizabeth believed in *the* Immaculate Conception? But, this issue of legitimacy remains prevalent in society. We've acclimated to single parent households and many of us have turned out well, but children still want to know who their fathers are. They want to have relationships with their fathers, *and their mothers*. When it is not possible, a hole begins to form. Nature abhors a vacuum and human nature will seek to fill the void. We must be very careful to protect those fragile places[13] and fill them with all good things.

Whereas matters of race and all of its accompanying social implications have been a significant part of my life experience, I do not place this perplexing issue at the intentional forefront for this book. However, it is my desire that perhaps lessons learned and shared will become a catalyst for healing the racial divide in America.

This short book encompasses so much territory, that even I am amazed at all the things God has brought me through. Yet, the title says it all. I have been Making Sweet Lemonade all my life. As I sit back and see what God has orchestrated, I have complete peace about every event, every memory, every line and word.

In closing, Making Sweet Lemonade's message is one of *healing*. It is the ability to seek the good in a seemingly bad situation. It is affectionately aspiring for the very best in life. *Making Sweet Lemonade is the ultimate art of resiliency.*

---

13   Proverbs 4:23

Above all else, guard thy heart
for out of it are the issues of life

— Proverbs 4:23

Much gratitude is extended to a number of individuals that provided reviews, editing, and loving support once this gift was ready for unveiling. I would be remiss to close the cover without thanking: Carolyn Mints, Cynthia Downs, Anne Serdula, Carmelita Byrd, Jeannine Klos, Sunya Folayan, Joyce Sewell, Mona Boykin, Tangela Davis, Melissa Holmes, Karen Norman, Dan Robinson, Robin Joiner, Leah Ponds, Dr. Laverne Daniels, Dr. Jeffrey Leak, and Dr. Clifford A. Jones, Sr.

The second printing of Making Sweet Lemonade will include a National Resource Directory to promote the safety and well-being of children. Any child and family advocacy agency, higher education foundation or support ministry that would like to be listed is encouraged to contact the author.

About The Author

Pat J. Schulz was born Josephine Schulz in Brooklyn, New York. Her formative years were divided between her birthplace and Lenoir, North Carolina. She obtained a B. S. degree in Business Administration from the University of North Carolina at Greensboro, and acquired Post Baccalaureate courses at the University of North Carolina at Charlotte in Psychology.

The majority of her professional experience has been in the insurance industry as a Financial Operations Manager. She obtained corporate certifications as a Diversity Trainer and Quality Management Administrator, earning top leadership awards for quality improvement application results.

As a former member of the American Business Women's Association, Schulz served numerous leadership roles and in 1994 was awarded the Charlotte Area ABWA Woman of the Year. She spearheaded the development of the Charlotte University Chapter scholarship foundation, during her term as chapter President.

As a community-service advocate, Schulz has served government appointments to North Carolina's Mecklenburg County Domestic Violence Advisory Board and the Women's Commission Advisory Board. Additional service contributions include the United Way (Loaned Executive, Allocations Board, Corporate Campaign Development and Speaker roles), MS Society Leadership Award, Kinder Mourne and The Council for Children Board of Directors. Additionally, Schulz has been certified as Bereavement and Loss lay-ministerial facilitator.

After having experienced personal restoration, Schulz combined her professional and community service experience to establish Personal Wellness Seminars — a program designed to assist others in attaining wholeness of mind, body and spirit.

She avails herself to speaking engagements on the effects of child exposure to domestic violence and has served a number of agencies in this capacity.

Schulz is presently a business consultant, the owner of ENHEART Publishing, and author of *Metamorphosis: A Life Journey* (1996).

For book signings, workshops and speaking engagements contact
pschulz@enheartpublishing.com

My Personal Library Resource Directory

Self Love	Dr. Robert Schular
Why Some Positive Thinkers Get Powerful Results	Norman Vincent Peale
My Mother / My Self	Nancy Friday
Motherless Daughters: The Legacy of Loss	Hope Eldeman
Whatever Happened to Daddy's Little Girl	Jonetta Rose Barris
The Color of Water	James McBride
Life on the Color Line	Gregory H. Williams
My Beautiful Broken Shell	Carol Hamblet Adams
Chosen Vessels	Rebecca Osaigbovo
Woman Thou Art Loosed	T.D. Jakes
Healing the Child Within	Charles Whitfield
Adult Children of Alcoholics	Janet Geringer Woititz
The Road Less Traveled	M. Scott Peck

These are books I've read over the years that were inspirational, motivational or educational aids, as I've sought to gather meaning of my life experiences. Perhaps they will also provide meaning to your journey.

Other Books

by ENHEART Publishing

Metamorphosis: A Life Journey	Pat J. Schulz
Marzetta Stood in for Mama	Glenda Horton Manning
Daddy Was a Big Man	Glenda Horton Manning
Saved?	Evangelist F.C. Fisher
Healing Truths	Anne P. Serdula
The Be Attitudes of Parenting	Glenda Horton Manning
There's a Little Boy on My Bed	Jeannine Klos